American English

# Personal Best

A1 Beginner

Student's Book and Workbook combined edition

A

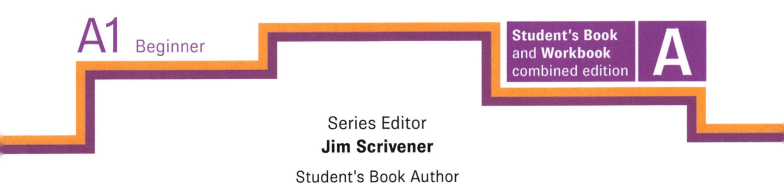

Series Editor
**Jim Scrivener**

Student's Book Author
**Graham Fruen**

Workbook Author
**Daniel Barber**

# STUDENT'S BOOK CONTENTS

Language App, unit-by-unit grammar and vocabulary games

# My life

## Hello

**1** ▶ 1.1   Read and listen. Match conversations 1–3 with pictures a–c.

**1** **Wendy** Good morning. Are you Emma, the new teacher?
**Emma** Yes, I am.
**Wendy** I'm Wendy. Nice to meet you. You're in Class 3.
**Emma** Thanks, Wendy. See you later.

**2** **Emma** Hello, I'm Emma. What's your name?
**Kiko** Hi, my name's Kiko.
**Emma** Nice to meet you, Kiko.
**Kiko** Are you a student here?
**Emma** No, I'm not. I'm your teacher!

**3** **Kiko** Emma, this is my friend, Misha.
**Emma** Hello. Hmm, you're not in Class 3, Misha.
**Misha** No, I'm in Class 4, and I'm late! Goodbye!
**Emma** Bye, Misha!

**2** Put the words from the conversations in the correct columns. Can you add any other words?

| Bye  Good morning  Hi  See you later | Hello | Goodbye |
| --- | --- | --- |

**3** **A** ▶ 1.2   Listen and repeat the highlighted phrases from the conversations in exercise 1. How do you say them in your language?

**B** Practice the conversations from exercise 1 in groups of four.

**4** **A** Complete the sentences with the words in the box. Then check your answers in the conversations.

| 're   'm   'm not   're not   Are |
| --- |

1 I _____ Wendy.
2 You _____ in Class 3.
3 _____ you a student here?

4 No, I _____ .
5 You _____ in Class 3, Misha.

**B** ▶ 1.3   Listen and repeat the contractions in **bold**. Then read the Grammar box.

1 I am = **I'm**      2 You are = **You're**      3 You are not = **You're not**

### 📖 Grammar   the verb *be* (*I, you*)

**Affirmative:**
***I'm*** *Wendy.*
***You're*** *in Class 4.*

**Negative:**
***You're not*** *in Class 3.*
***I'm not*** *a student.*

**Questions and short answers:**
***Are you*** *a teacher?*
*Yes,* ***I am.***    *No,* ***I'm not.***

**Go to Grammar practice:** the verb *be* (*I, you*), page 96

**5**  **A** ▶1.5   Complete the conversation. Listen and check.

> **Kiko**  Hello. What's ¹_____ name?
> **Eleni**  ²_____ name's Eleni.
> **Kiko**  Nice to ³_____ you, Eleni. I ⁴_____ Kiko.
> **Eleni**  Nice to meet you, Kiko. ⁵_____ you a student here?
> **Kiko**  ⁶ Yes, I _____ .

**B** In pairs, practice the conversation using your names.

**6**  Introduce yourself and your partner to another pair.
  **A**  *Hello, I'm Caro. This is Pablo.*
  **B**  *Nice to meet you. My name's Malika, and this is Petra.*

**7**  ▶1.6   Read the phrases and write *Teacher* or *Student*. Listen and check.

1 _____

**Open your books.**

2 _____

**Excuse me, what does "late" mean?**

3 _____

**I'm sorry, I don't understand.**

4 _____

**Listen and repeat.**

5 _____

**How do you say "buenos días" in English?**

6 _____

**Work in pairs.**

**Go to Vocabulary practice:** classroom language, page 106

**8**  ▶1.8   **Pronunciation:** the alphabet  Listen and repeat the sounds, words, and letters.

| /ey/ | /iy/ | /e/ | /ay/ | /ow/ | /uw/ | /ɑ/ |
|------|------|-----|------|------|------|-----|
| late | meet | yes | my | no | you | pasta |
| Aa  Hh  Jj  Kk | Bb  Cc  Dd  Ee<br>Gg  Pp  Tt  Vv<br>Zz | Ff  Ll  Mm  Nn<br>Ss  Xx | Ii  Yy | Oo | Qq  Uu  Ww | Rr |

**9**  ▶1.9   Listen to the conversations. Write the names of the students.

**Class 3**
Student names:
1 _____
2 _____
3 _____

**ABC**
ABC School of English

**Go to Communication practice:** Student A page 134, Student B page 142

**10**  Introduce yourself to five students. Ask the questions and write the answers.

What's your name?   How do you spell that?

**Personal Best**   Write a conversation between a teacher and a new student.

## 1A Where's she from?

**1 A** In pairs, match the flags with the countries.

**A** *What's flag "a"?* **B** *I think it's Mexico.*

 c

 d

 e

 f

 g

 h

| 1 Argentina ____ | 3 China ____ | 5 Spain ____ | 7 the UK ____ |
| 2 Brazil ____ | 4 Mexico ____ | 6 Turkey ____ | 8 the U.S. ____ |

**B** ▶ 1.10 Listen, check, and repeat.

**2 A** ▶ 1.11 Listen to the conversation. Repeat it in pairs.

> **A** Where are you from?    **A** Where's Salta?
> **B** I'm from Salta.    **B** It's in Argentina.

**B** In pairs, practice the conversation using the cities and countries.

> Toledo / Spain   Izmir / Turkey   Harbin / China   York / the UK

> I'm from the UK.
> I'm British.

**3** Look at the picture. Match the countries from exercise 1 with the nationalities.

| 1 British _the UK_ | 4 American _____ | 7 Turkish _____ |
| 2 Spanish _____ | 5 Argentinian _____ | 8 Brazilian _____ |
| 3 Mexican _____ | 6 Chinese _____ | |

**Personal Best**

**Go to Vocabulary practice:** countries and nationalities, page 107

**4** ▶ 1.13 Do the quiz in pairs. Listen and check.

# THE COUNTRIES QUIZ

**1** **What nationality is Meghan Markle?**
  **a** She's British.
  **b** She's American.

**5** **Which sentence is correct?**
  **a** Sydney is the capital of Australia.
  **b** Sydney's not the capital of Australia.

**2** **Where is Mount Fuji?**
  **a** It's in China.
  **b** It's in Japan.

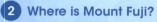

**6** **Is *ceviche* Mexican or Peruvian?**
  **a** It's Mexican.
  **b** It's Peruvian.

**3** **Is this elephant from India or Africa?**
  **a** It's from India.
  **b** It's from Africa.

**7** **Where is the Bosphorus?**
  **a** It's in Turkey.
  **b** It's in Russia.

**4** **Is Selena Gómez Russian?**
  **a** Yes, she is.
  **b** No, she's not.

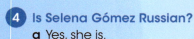

**8** **What nationality is Paulo Coelho?**
  **a** He's Italian.
  **b** He's Brazilian.

**5 A** Match the pronouns *he*, *she*, and *it* with the people and things.

1 he  a Selena Gómez
2 she  b *ceviche*
3 it  c Paulo Coelho

**B** Check (✔) the form of the verb *be* that we use with *he*, *she*, and *it*. Then read the Grammar box.

1 am ☐   2 is ☐   3 are ☐

📖 **Grammar**   the verb *be* (*he*, *she*, *it*)

| Affirmative: | Negative: | Questions and short answers: |
|---|---|---|
| He**'s** Japanese. | Barcelona **isn't** the capital of Spain. | **Is** it from India? |
| She**'s** from Mexico. | She**'s not** Australian. / She **isn't** Australian. | Yes, it **is**.   No, it**'s not**. / No, it **isn't**. |

**Go to Grammar practice:** the verb *be* (*he*, *she*, *it*), page 96

**6 A** ▶ 1.15  **Pronunciation:** word stress  Listen and repeat the words. Pay attention to the underlined stressed syllables.

Ja<u>pan</u>   Japa<u>nese</u>   <u>Mex</u>ico   <u>Mex</u>ican   <u>Ita</u>ly   I<u>ta</u>lian   <u>Tur</u>key   <u>Turk</u>ish

**B** ▶ 1.16  Underline the stress in the countries and nationalities. Then listen, check, and repeat.

1 I'm Brazilian.   2 She's from Germany.   3 It's Chinese.   4 Is he from Argentina?

**7** In pairs, ask and answer the question *Where's … from?* about the people and things.

**A** *Where's Zara from?*   **B** *Is it Italian?*
**A** *No, it's not. It's Spanish.*

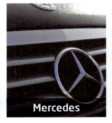

| Zara | Ryan Gosling | Mercedes | Thalía | Neymar | Chow mein |

**8 A** ▶ 1.17  Listen and repeat the numbers.

| 0 | 1 | 2 | 3 | 4 | 5 | 6 | 7 | 8 | 9 | 10 |
|---|---|---|---|---|---|---|---|---|---|---|
| zero/oh | one | two | three | four | five | six | seven | eight | nine | ten |

**B** ▶ 1.18  What are the country calling codes? Listen and write the answers.

1 China  + _____
2 Colombia  + _____
3 India  + _____
4 Mexico  + _____
5 Spain  + _____
6 Turkey  + _____

**Go to Communication practice:** Student A page 134, Student B page 142

**9 A** In pairs, write six more quiz questions about countries and nationalities.

**B** Work with another pair. Ask and answer your quiz questions.

**A** *What is the capital of Peru? a) It's Lima. b) It's Bogotá.*
**B** *It's not Bogotá – that's in Colombia. I think it's Lima.*
**A** *That's right! Your turn.*

## 1B Welcome to *Learning Curve*!

**1** Match the jobs in the box with pictures a–f.

doctor   engineer   office worker   police officer   taxi driver   waiter

**Go to Vocabulary practice:** jobs, page 108

**2 A** ▶ 1.20   Look at the picture. Listen and complete the conversation.

**A** What's my job?
**B** Are you an [1]_____ ?
**A** No, I'm not. Try again!
**B** Are you a [2]_____ ?
**A** Yes, I am.

**B** In pairs, play "What's my job?"

**3** ▶ 1.21   Watch or listen to the start of a webshow called *Learning Curve*. Match the cities with the people.

1   New York          a   Simon, Kate, Marina
2   London            b   Ethan, Penny, Mohammed, Marc

| **Skill** | **listening for information about people** |
| --- | --- |

**We often listen to information about people.**
- Don't worry if you don't understand everything the speakers say.
- Read the questions and think about the information you need to listen for: name, job, nationality, etc.
- Listen for the verb *be*: *I'm … / He's … / She's …* etc.

**4** ▶ 1.21   Read the Skill box. Watch or listen again, and choose the correct information about the people.

**Simon Collins**
Nationality: British
Job: [1] *TV host / receptionist*

**Ethan Moore**
Nationality:
[2] *American / British*
Job: TV host

**Penny Abernathy**
Nationality:
English and
[3] *Italian / Argentinian*
Job: TV host

**Marina Ivanova**
Nationality: Russian
Job: [4] *receptionist / teacher*

**Mohammed Bensallem**
Nationality: American
Job: [5] *TV host / office worker*

**Marc Kim**
Nationality: *American*
Job: [6] *doctor / IT specialist*

**Kate McRea**
Nationality: [7] *American / Argentinian*
Job: TV host

**5** ▶1.22 Watch or listen to the rest of the show. Who's not in London now? Where is he/she?

Viktor

Sarah

Pedro

**6** ▶1.22 Watch or listen again. Complete the information with countries and jobs.
1 Viktor: from: _____   job: _____ and _____
2 Sarah: from: _____   job: _____
3 Pedro: from: _____   job: _____

**7** **A** In pairs, ask and answer the questions about the three people.

Where is … from?   What's his/her job?

**B** In pairs, ask and answer the questions about you.

Where are you from?   What's your job?

**8** ▶1.23 Listen and read what Kate says. How does she say the contractions in **bold**? What do they mean?

> Hi, **I'm** Kate from *Learning Curve*. **What's** your name?

**Listening builder**   **contractions**

In English, we often use contractions, especially when we speak.
***I'm*** from the United States. = ***I am*** from the United States.
***She's*** not a student. = ***She is*** not a student.
***What's*** your job? = ***What is*** your job?

**9** ▶1.24 Read the Listening builder. Listen and write the contractions.
1 _____ Spanish.   3 He _____ a doctor.   5 _____ an engineer.
2 _____ your name?   4 _____ from Japan.   6 The _____ here.

**10** ▶1.25 In pairs, look at the pictures of Jia and Luis. Guess the information about the people. Listen to the conversations and check.

job?   nationality?   Where now?

Jia

Luis

**11** Write the names of three friends or members of your family. In pairs, ask and answer questions about them.

**A** *Where's Saanvi from?*   **B** *She's from Nagpur.*
**A** *What's her job?*   **B** *She's an IT worker.*
**A** *Where is she now?*   **B** *She's in Mumbai.*

**Personal Best** Choose five classmates and write their jobs, e.g., *Carla's a teacher.*

## 1C We are the champions

**1** **A** Write the numbers in the box in the correct order.

> sixteen thirteen fourteen seventeen twelve twenty ~~eleven~~ fifteen nineteen eighteen
>
> *eleven,* _____

**B** Look at the pictures and read the numbers. Check (✔) the numbers that are correct.

1 twenty-three ☐   2 fifty-four ☐   3 eighty-six ☐   4 sixty-eight ☐   5 one hundred ☐   6 thirty ☐

**Go to Vocabulary practice:** numbers 0–100, page 111

**2** **A** In pairs, ask and answer the question *How old is …?* for the people in the picture.

**A** *How old is Kyle?*   **B** *I think he's 40.*

**B** ▶1.27 Listen and write the ages.

Kyle _____   Martin _____   Lorna _____

Kyle    Martin    Lorna

**3** **A** Look at the picture. What do you know about the rock band Queen? Do you know any songs or the names of the band members?

**B** Read the introduction to the interview. What is the name of the band?

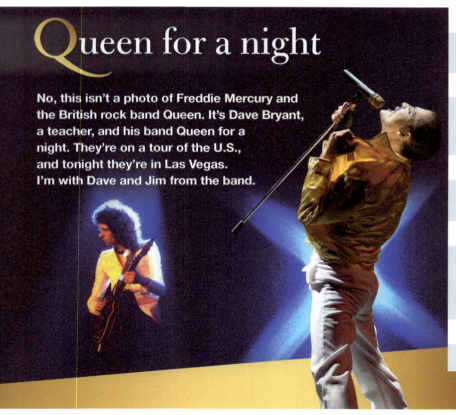

# Queen for a night

No, this isn't a photo of Freddie Mercury and the British rock band Queen. It's Dave Bryant, a teacher, and his band Queen for a night. They're on a tour of the U.S., and tonight they're in Las Vegas. I'm with Dave and Jim from the band.

**So Jim, are you all teachers?**

**Jim**  No, we're not. I'm an engineer, and Ed and Mick are doctors.

**And where are you from?**

**Dave**  I'm from New York, Jim and Ed are from Boston, and Mick's from Atlantic City. We're old friends from college.

**How's the tour going?**

**Jim**  It's good, but it's hard. It's a big tour – fourteen cities – and we're not so young now!

**Really? How old are you?**

**Dave**  Mick and I are forty-seven. And you and Ed are fifty …

**Jim**  I'm not fifty! Ed's fifty … I'm forty-nine.

**Dave**  Oh yeah. Sorry, Jim!

**And what's your favorite Queen song?**

**Dave**  That's easy! It's *We Are the Champions*!

**4** ▶ 1.28 Read and listen to the interview. Complete the information about the band.

|  | Dave | Jim | Ed | Mick |
|---|---|---|---|---|
| job |  |  |  |  |
| city |  |  |  |  |
| age |  |  |  |  |

**5** **A** Read the sentences from the interview. Match the people in **bold** with the pronouns *we*, *you*, and *they*.

**1** **Mick and I** are forty-seven. _____    **2** **Jim and Ed** are from Boston. _____    **3** And **you and Ed** are fifty. _____

**B** Check (✔) the form of the verb *be* we use when we talk about more than one person. Then read the Grammar box.

**a** *am / am not* ☐       **b** *is / is not* ☐       **c** *are / are not* ☐

**Grammar**    **the verb *be* (*we*, *you*, *they*)**

**Affirmative:**
*We're old friends.*
*They're on a tour of the U.S.*

**Negative:**
*We're not young.*
*They're not the rock band Queen.*

**Questions and short answers:**
*Are you all teachers?*
*Yes, we are.    No, we're not.*

Go to Grammar practice: the verb *be* (*we*, *you*, *they*), page 96

**6** **A** ▶ 1.30 **Pronunciation:** numbers  Listen and repeat the numbers. Pay attention to how the stress changes.

**1 a** thir<u>teen</u>    **b** <u>thir</u>ty    **2 a** four<u>teen</u>    **b** <u>for</u>ty    **3 a** <u>fif</u>teen    **b** <u>fif</u>ty

**B** ▶ 1.31 Listen and check (✔) the numbers you hear. Listen again and repeat.

**1 a** He's not 16. ☐    **b** He's not 60. ☐    **3 a** We're not 17. ☐    **b** We're not 70. ☐
**2 a** She's 18. ☐    **b** She's 80. ☐    **4 a** They're 19. ☐    **b** They're 90. ☐

Go to Communication practice: Student A page 134, Student B page 142

**7** Match adjectives 1–4 from the interview with their opposites in the box.

bad  small  old  difficult

**1** young _____    **2** good _____    **3** big _____    **4** easy _____

Go to Vocabulary practice: adjectives (1), page 109

**8** Describe the pictures in pairs. Use affirmative and negative forms.

*Picture a: They're big. They're not small.*

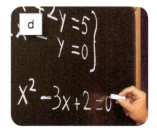

**9** **A** In small groups, imagine you are in a band and complete the chart.

| The name of the band | Your names | Your ages | Nationalities |
|---|---|---|---|
|  |  |  |  |

**B** Work with another group. Interview each other about your bands.

What's the name of your band?    What are your names?    How old are you?    Where are you from?

**Personal Best**  Write a short paragraph about a band you like.

## 1D What's your e-mail address?

**1** Match the places in the box with pictures a–c.

hotel   car rental office   gym

**2 A** Look at the form. Match it with one of the pictures in exercise 1.

**B** ▶ 1.33 Listen to the conversation. Which piece of information in the form is **incorrect**?

### Customer Information

*CARS-4-U*

| Title | MR. ☐  MS. ☑  MRS. ☐ | | |
|---|---|---|---|
| Last name | Martín | First name(s) | Luisa |
| Nationality | Mexican | Date of birth | 06/17/1980 |
| Street address | Calle de la Paz, 65, Puebla, Mexico | | |
| Zip code | 72160 | | |
| e-mail address | luisa.martin@mymail.com | | |
| Phone number | 52-222-266-5647 | | |

🔧 **Skill**  **filling out a form**

**When you fill out a form, read all the instructions and sections carefully.**

• Use the correct *title*. *Mr.* = a man, *Ms.* = a woman (married or unmarried), *Mrs.* = a married woman.
• Your *last name* is your family name.
• Write your *date of birth* in numbers: the month/the day/the year: *09/13/1995*.
• For e-mail addresses: @ = "at" and .com = "dot com."

**3** Read the Skill box. Match sections 1–9 with information a–i.

| | | | |
|---|---|---|---|
| 1 | zip code | a | Taylor |
| 2 | date of birth | b | 17401 |
| 3 | street address | c | Mr. |
| 4 | last name | d | c.taylor@candb.com |
| 5 | first name | e | 717-322-5623 |
| 6 | e-mail address | f | 11/23/1988 |
| 7 | title | g | American |
| 8 | phone number | h | Carl |
| 9 | nationality | i | 3927 Stout Street, York, PA |

**4** In pairs, ask and answer questions about you, using the information in exercise 3.

A *What's your last name?*    B *It's Taylor.*
A *How do you spell that?*    B *It's T-A-Y-L-O-R.*

**5** Look at answers a–i in exercise 3. Check (✔) the information with capital letters.

1 first name ☐    3 e-mail address ☐    5 street ☐
2 last name ☐     4 nationality ☐       6 city ☐

---

**Text builder    capital letters**

**In English, we use capital letters (*A, B, C, D,* etc.) for the following:**
- the first word in a sentence: *What's your name?*
- the personal pronoun *I*: *Hello, I'm Robert.*
- the names of people and places: *Emma is from Boston.*
- countries, nationalities, and languages: *We're from China. We're Chinese.*

---

**6 A** Read the Text builder. Find one **incorrect** capital letter in each sentence.

1 My friend Lena is American. She's From Florida.
2 Hello, I'm Antonio. I'm a new Student.
3 Our street Address is 8927 North Winery Ave, Austin, TX 73301.
4 This is Mesut. He's from Turkey and he's Twenty-one.

**B** Rewrite the sentences with capital letters.

1 what's his job? is he a doctor?                          _____
2 my street address is 11004 spruce run, san diego, ca 92131.    _____
3 they aren't from germany. they're from poland.          _____
4 i'm your new english teacher. my name's jack.           _____

**7 A** **PREPARE** Look at the form. Be sure that you understand all the information you need to write.

**ATLAS HOTEL**

**Customer Information**

| Title | Mr. ☐ | Ms. ☐ | Other ☐ |
|---|---|---|---|

Last name        _____
First name(s)    _____
Date of birth    _____
Nationality      _____
Street address   _____
Zip code         _____
E-mail address   _____
Phone number     _____

**B** **PRACTICE** Fill out your form. Remember to use capital letters correctly.

**C** **PERSONAL BEST** Exchange forms with a partner. Is it clear and easy to read? Are the capital letters correct?

# People and things

## 2A The man with only 15 things

**1** ▶ 2.1 In pairs, match the words in the box with objects a–f. Listen and check.

a book   a purse   keys   a watch   an umbrella   a camera

a    b    c    d    e    f

Personal Best

**Go to Vocabulary practice:** personal items, page 110

**2** Look at exercise 1 and answer the questions. Then read the Grammar box.

1 Which noun do we use with *an*? _____    2 Which noun is plural? _____

| 📖 **Grammar** | **singular and plural nouns** | |
|---|---|---|
| **Singular nouns:** | *a key* | *an umbrella* | *a watch* |
| **Plural nouns:** | *keys* | *umbrellas* | *watches* |

Personal Best

**Go to Grammar practice:** singular and plural nouns, page 97

**3** **A** Imagine you live with only 15 things. What are your 15 things?

**B** Read the text. Are your 15 things the same as Andrew's?

*This Book is About*
**TRAVEL**
A MODERN MANUAL
15 COUNTRIES
WITH 15 THINGS
**ANDREW HYDE**

# 15 countries *with* 15 things

This is Andrew Hyde, and that's his book: *15 countries with 15 things*. Andrew is from Colorado in the U.S., and he's a writer and traveler. And it's true – he's a man with only 15 things!

**THESE ARE HIS 15 THINGS:**

| | | |
|---|---|---|
| 1 ___ backpack | 6 ___ wallet | 13 ___ shoes |
| 2 ___ smartphone | 7 ___ jacket | 14 ___ towel |
| 3 ___ camera | 8 ___ pants | 15 ___ toiletry bag |
| 4 ___ iPad | 9 & 10 ___ shirts | |
| 5 ___ sunglasses | 11 & 12 ___ shorts | |

Andrew is back in the U.S. now, but is he happy with just those 15 things? Yes, he says. Life is easy without a lot of things.

**4** Look at the list of Andrew's things again. Write *a* or *an* for singular nouns, and – for plural nouns.

**5** Complete the sentences from the text with the pronouns in the box. Which words do we use with singular nouns? Which ones with plural nouns? Then read the Grammar box.

| that | those | this | these |
|------|-------|------|-------|

**1** _____ is Andrew Hyde.        **3** _____ are his 15 things.
**2** _____'s his book.            **4** Is he happy with just _____ 15 things?

> 📖 **Grammar**   *this, that, these, those*
>
> **Things that are near us:**          **Things that aren't near us:**
> **This** is my purse.                 **That**'s my car.
> **These** are my keys.                **Those** are my friends.

*Personal Best*

**Go to Grammar practice:** *this, that, these, those,* page 97

**6 A** ▶ **2.5** **Pronunciation:** the /ɪ/ and /iy/ sounds  Listen and repeat the sounds and words.

/ɪ/   this    it    is      six
/iy/  these   he    three   keys

**B** ▶ **2.6**  In pairs, say the sentences. Listen, check, and repeat.

**1** This is my city.               **3** Is that tree Japanese?
**2** These are my keys.            **4** She's six and he's three.

**Go to Communication practice:** Students A and B page 135

**7** Choose the correct words to complete the text.

## What's in your bag?

**Maria Clara, office worker, Rio de Janeiro**
[1] *This / These* is my purse and [2] *this / these* are my things. This [3] *is / are* my book. It's in English! [4] *These / That* are my keys. [5] *This / These* key is for my house and [6] *that / those* key is for my car. [7] *This is / That's* my car over there – it's [8] *a / an* sports car! What's this? It's [9] *a / an* umbrella. It's very small! And the last thing? These are [10] *a / –* sunglasses!

**8 A** ▶ **2.7**  Listen and match conversations 1–3 with pictures a–c.

**B** ▶ **2.7**  Complete the phrases from the conversations with *this, that, these,* and *those.* Listen again and check.

**1** Jack    What's _____ ?              Helen   _____ is my purse.
**2** Woman   Jorge, who's _____ over there?   Jorge   _____'s Sergio.
**3** Man     Hi, Karen. What are _____ ?       Karen   _____ are my cameras.

**9** Put some things from your purse or backpack on the desk. In pairs, ask and answer questions about the things.

**A** *What's that?*     **B** *This is a book. It's in Spanish.*     **A** *And what are those?*     **B** *These are my keys.*

**Personal Best**   Write about the things in your purse or backpack, as in exercise 7.

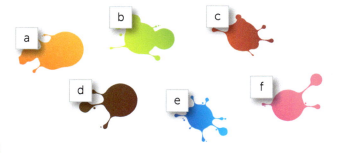

## 2B Lost!

Personal Best

**1 A** Match the words in the box with the colors.

blue   brown   green   orange   pink   red

**Go to Vocabulary practice:** colors, page 110

**B** In pairs, point to items in the classroom. Ask and answer *What color is that/are those...?*

**A** *What color are those books?*   **B** *They're orange.*

---

🔧 **Skill** | **preparing to read**

**Before you read a text, look at other information to help you prepare.**
- Think about the style of the text. Is it from a magazine, a website, a letter?
- Look at the pictures. What people, places, and things can you see?
- Read the title. What does it mean?

---

**2 A** Read the Skill box. What do you think the text on page 17 is about? Check (✔) a, b, or c.

**a** lost tourists in London ☐   **b** transportation in London ☐   **c** lost items in London ☐

**B** Read the text quickly and check your answer.

**3** Read the text again. Are the sentences true (T) or false (F)?

1  The Lost and Found Office is in London. _____
2  The items are all from buses. _____
3  Tim Carlisle is a tour guide every day. _____
4  The laptop is new. _____
5  All the musical instruments are expensive. _____
6  The $15,000 is in the office now. _____

**4** Complete the sentences with the words in the box. Check your answers in the text.

expensive   violin   guitars   cheap

1  These _____ are _____ .
2  That's an _____ _____ .

---

🧩 **Text builder** | **adjectives and nouns**

**adjective + noun:**  $15,000 in a **brown envelope**.
**noun + be + adjective:**  This **laptop is new**.

**Look!** Adjectives don't change with plural nouns: *It's an **expensive instrument**. They're **expensive instruments**.*

---

**5** Read the Text builder. Put the words in order to make sentences.

1  good  it's  a  camera  _____
2  sunglasses  they're  expensive  _____
3  green  purse  the  is  _____
4  are  the  brown  wallets  _____
5  fast  a  it's  car  _____

**6 A** ▶ 2.9  Read and listen to the conversation in a Lost and Found Office.

**B** In pairs, change the highlighted words and make a new conversation.

**A** Hello, can I help you?
**B** Do you have my wallet? It's a small, black wallet. It's expensive.
**A** Hold on. Is this your wallet?
**B** Yes, that's it!

# Lost in London

22,000 cell phones, 12,000 credit cards, a green "Incredible Hulk" toy, $15,000 in a brown envelope …

These are some of the things in the Transportation for London Lost and Found Office. Every year, 300,000 items are lost on buses, trains, and taxis in the city. I'm at the office in central London, and with me is Tim Carlisle. Tim is an employee here, but today he's my tour guide.

"Look at all these things – wallets, glasses, purses, backpacks, shoes, cell phones – they're all here," Tim tells me. "Look at this laptop – it's new."

In a different part of the office are musical instruments. "These guitars are cheap, but that's an expensive violin," he says.

"What's over there?" I ask.

"Those are umbrellas. Big umbrellas, small umbrellas, blue umbrellas, pink umbrellas …"

"And what about the envelope with $15,000?" I ask. "Is it still here?"

"No," Tim says. "An old man collected it last month. He's 80 years old and he doesn't like banks!"

And that's the end of my tour. It's time for me to go. Now, where's my phone?

## 2C My family

**1** Match the people in the box with pictures a–d.

husband and wife   mother and son   father and daughter   brother and sister

**2** Put the words from exercise 1 in the correct columns.

| Male ♂ | Female ♀ |
|--------|----------|
| *brother* | *sister* |

**Go to Vocabulary practice:** family and friends, page 111

**3 A** Discuss the questions in pairs.

1 Are you from a big family or a small family?
2 Do you live with your family?
3 Does anyone in your family live in a different city or country?

**B** Read the text quickly. What is Laura's family situation? Is she sad about it?

# Long-distance families

Are you part of a "long-distance" family? Are your brothers or sisters in a different city or country? Are you a long way from your parents or children? Tell us your stories.

### Laura Wickham

Hi! My name's Laura. My husband Seamus and I are long-distance parents! We live in Cork in Ireland. Our daughter Amy is 30 years old, and she's in Australia. Our son Conor is 26 years old, and he's in the U.S. Amy and Conor are a long distance from us, but their lives are very interesting. Amy's an IT worker in Perth. Her husband Pete is from there. He's an engineer. Conor's a surfing teacher in Los Angeles. He loves California and its beautiful beaches, so it's his dream job! Conor's girlfriend Nicole is a Hollywood actor … well, that's her dream. Right now, she's a waitress.
We're on Skype a lot with our children, but it's difficult with the time differences. Am I sad that they're so far away? Sometimes, but the important thing is that they're happy.

**4** Read the text again. Match the information with the people.

1 This person is 30 years old.          **a** Seamus
2 This person is a waitress.            **b** Amy
3 This person lives in Cork.            **c** Pete
4 This person is a surfing teacher.     **d** Conor
5 This person is Australian.            **e** Nicole

**5** Complete the sentences from the text with the words in the box.

> our   my   her   its   his   their

1 _____ name's Laura.
2 _____ son Conor is 26 years old.
3 _____ lives are very interesting.
4 _____ husband Pete is from there.
5 He loves California and _____ beautiful beaches.
6 It's _____ dream job!

**6 A** Choose the correct option to complete the sentence from the text.

*Conor's / Pete's / Seamus's* girlfriend Nicole is a Hollywood actor.

**B** What ending do we add to names and nouns to show possession? Read the Grammar box.

---

📖 **Grammar**   **possessive adjectives, 's for possession**

**Possessive adjectives:**

| I | my: | *I'm a teacher.* **My** *name's Karen.* |
| you | your: | *Are you OK?* **Your** *phone's broken.* |
| he | his: | *He's a tour guide.* **His** *job's interesting.* |
| she | her: | *She's Chinese, but* **her** *husband's British.* |
| it | its: | *Sydney's a great city.* **Its** *beaches are beautiful.* |
| we | our: | *We're in Class 3, and* **our** *teacher's very good!* |
| they | their: | *Jo and Ben aren't here. They're in* **their** *car.* |

**'s for possession:**

**Kim's** *mother is from Germany.*
*Is this* **Amy's** *book?*
**My son's** *new phone is expensive.*

---

Go to Grammar practice: possessive adjectives, 's for possession, page 97

**7 A** ▶ 2.12 **Pronunciation:** *'s* Listen and repeat. Pay attention to the *'s* sound.

son's        daughter's        Amy's        Conor's        my husband's        my sister's

**B** ▶ 2.13 In pairs, say the sentences. Then listen, check, and repeat.

1 My husband's name is Felipe.
2 Our son's girlfriend is French.
3 My wife's parents are from Canada.
4 Sara's brother's girlfriend is a doctor.

Go to Communication practice: Student A page 135, Student B page 143

**8** ▶ 2.14 Look at the people. In pairs, guess their relationship. Listen and check.

**A** *I think Jim is Tom Hanks's son.*        **B** *Yes, or maybe he's his brother.*

| Tom Hanks  | Victoria Beckham  | Will Smith  | Shakira  | Andy Murray  |
| Jim Hanks 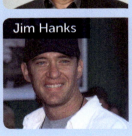 | Louise Adams  | Jaden Smith  | Gerard Piqué  | Judy Murray  |

**9** Choose five people in your family and write down their names. In pairs, ask and answer questions about the people.

**A** *Who is Azra?*        **B** *She's my brother's wife.*

> Who is he/she?      How old is he/she?      What is his/her job?

Learning Curve

## 2D What time is it?

**1 A** ▶ 2.15 In pairs, match the times in the box with the clocks. Listen and check.

> five o'clock   eight ten   quarter after/past ten   six thirty   eleven forty-five   three fifty-five

1 _____  2 _____  3 _____  4 _____  5 _____  6 _____

**B** ▶ 2.16 Complete the times. Listen, check, and repeat.

1  It's eleven _____ .
2  It's _____ three.
3  It's twelve _____ .
4  It's eight _____ .

**2 A** ▶ 2.17 Watch or listen to the start of *Learning Curve*. Choose the correct options to complete the sentences.

1  Kate is _____ .
   a  at home       b  on vacation       c  at work
2  _____ are talking on the telephone.
   a  Kate's parents   b  Kate's friends   c  Kate's brothers
3  They are in _____ .
   a  Boston       b  Los Angeles       c  London
4  Kate has _____ and a sister.
   a  no brothers   b  one brother   c  two brothers

**B** ▶ 2.17 Watch or listen again, and answer the questions.

1  What time is it in London?       _____
2  What time is it in Los Angeles?   _____

| **Conversation builder** | telling the time |
| --- | --- |

**Asking for the time:**
*What time is it?*       *What time's the movie?*
*What's the time?*       *What time's the next bus?*

**Talking about times:**
*It's ten o'clock.*       *The movie is at eight thirty.*
*It's seven a.m./p.m.*   *The bus is in ten minutes.*

**3 A** Read the Conversation builder. Match the questions with pictures a–d.

a    b    c    d

1  What's the time?                    _____
2  What time is CSI Miami?             _____
3  What time is it in New York?        _____
4  What time's the train to Stamford?  _____

**B** Ask and answer the questions in pairs.

**4** ▶ 2.18 Watch or listen to the rest of the show. Match the times in the box with the people.

8:15   9:00   3:00   8:45   12:30

Man 1

Woman 1

Woman 2

Man 2

Simon

**5 A** ▶ 2.18 Match the questions with the people from exercise 4. Watch or listen again, and check.

1 When's the game? _____
2 OK, what time is it? _____
3 Excuse me. What time's the *James Bond* movie? _____
4 Excuse me. What time is it, please? _____
5 Where's the number 67 bus? _____

**B** Which questions are polite? Why?

🔧 **Skill**   **asking for information politely**

**When you ask for information, it's important to be polite.**
- Use *Excuse me* to get the person's attention.
- At the end of the conversation, say *Thank you* or *Thanks*.
- If you want to be extra polite, say *Please* at the end of questions.

**6** ▶ 2.19 Read the Skill box. In pairs, guess the missing words from the conversations. Listen and check.

| | |
|---|---|
| **Woman 1** ¹_____ . What time is it, ²_____ ? | **Woman 2** ⁴_____ , what time is the number 67 bus? |
| **Kate** It's 8:15. Quarter past. | **Kate** Next bus ... 8:45. It's in ten minutes. |
| **Woman 1** Oh! I'm late. ³_____ very much. | **Woman 2** Oh, 8:45, not 8:35. Ten minutes. OK. ⁵_____ . |

**7** In pairs, practice asking for information politely.

| Questions | Answers |
|---|---|
| what / the teacher's name | It's Leanne. |
| what time / next bus to Chicago | It's at 12:20 p.m. |
| where / the museum | It's that building. |
| what / name of this restaurant | It's The Golden Dragon. |
| what / the school's phone number | It's 354 269. |

**Go to Communication practice:** Student A page 135, Student B page 143

**8 A** PREPARE In pairs, choose the movie theater or the airport and invent the missing information.

★ SILVER MOVIE THEATER ★

| MOVIE TITLE | TIME | SCREEN |
|---|---|---|
| Star Wars | _____ | _____ |
| Titanic | _____ | _____ |
| The Wizard of Oz | _____ | _____ |

**Airport departures** ✈   10:05

| Flight | Time | Gate |
|---|---|---|
| Stockholm | _____ | _____ |
| Beijing | _____ | _____ |
| Lima | _____ | _____ |

**B** PRACTICE In pairs, ask and answer questions about the movies or the flights. Remember to be polite.

**C** PERSONAL BEST Invent information for the other situation and repeat the activity. Is your speaking better this time?

**Personal Best** Write a conversation with a tourist in your local train or bus station.

# Grammar

**1** Choose the correct options to complete the sentences.

1 Hi Laura, I _____ Khalid's brother. Nice to meet you.
   a 's
   b 're
   c 'm

2 How old _____ your grandfather?
   a are
   b is
   c am

3 _____ these your glasses?
   a Am
   b Is
   c Are

4 A Is your sister's boyfriend from Brazil?
   B No, _____ .
   a he's not
   b she's not
   c I'm not

5 A What's this?
   B It's _____ old book.
   a –
   b a
   c an

6 _____ my mother over there with the blue umbrella.
   a These are
   b This is
   c That's

7 My wife's a chef, and this is _____ new restaurant.
   a she's
   b her
   c his

8 My _____ last name is Chen.
   a grandfather's
   b grandfather
   c grandfathers

**2** Rewrite the sentences with the new words.

1 He's an English teacher.
   They *'re English teachers* .

2 These are my red pens.
   This _____ .

3 We're happy with our new tablets.
   I _____ .

4 Those expensive cars are Italian.
   That _____ .

5 I'm a student in India.
   She _____ .

6 My brother's an office worker, and this is his backpack.
   My brothers _____ , and
   these _____ .

**3** Choose the correct options to complete the text.

**A HOLLYWOOD FAMILY**

[1] *These / This* is Zooey Deschanel. She's [2] *a / an* actor and a singer. [3] *She / Her* sister Emily is an actor, too. She's in the TV show *Bones*. What [4] *'s / 're* their mother's job? An actor. And [5] *their / our* father's job? [6] *Her / His* job is in movies too! That's not all – Zooey's [7] *sister's / sisters* husband is … an actor. They [8] *'re / 's* from California in the U.S., and they're a Hollywood family. They [9] *are / 're not* the only family like this. From Marlon Brando's family to Will Smith's family, they [10] *'m / 're* easy to find in Hollywood.

# Vocabulary

**1** Put the words in the box in the correct columns.

difficult engineer grandfather interesting
IT worker cell phone mother pencil
receptionist small watch wife

| Jobs | Adjectives | Family | Personal items |
|------|-----------|--------|----------------|
|      | *difficult* |       |                |

**2** Circle the word that is different. Explain your answers.

1  black      new        orange     gold
2  chef       tour guide  TV host    grandmother
3  French     Polish     Russian    Canada
4  fifty      thirteen   fourteen   seventeen
5  son        glasses    change     keys
6  Hi         Bye        Hello      Good morning
7  bad        boring     ugly       happy
8  father     daughter   boyfriend  husband

**3** Choose the correct options to complete the sentences.

1  Jing Wei is _____ . She's from Shanghai.
   a doctor          b Chinese          c brother
2  Excuse me, what does "building" _____ ?
   a say             b understand       c mean
3  My sister's daughter is six, and her _____ is four.
   a son             b children         c husband
4  That camera is very _____ .
   a new             b young            c sad
5  Russia is a very _____ country.
   a small           b easy             c big
6  I'm from _____ . I'm American.
   a the UK          b the U.S.         c Argentina
7  A  It's nine fifteen.
   B  Sorry I'm _____ .
   a student         b teacher          c late
8  Macu is a _____ . She's in her car all day.
   a salesclerk      b taxi driver      c girlfriend
9  A  What color is a chef's hat?
   B  It's _____ .
   a white           b small            c pink
10 The pages of this old _____ are yellow.
   a tablet          b wallet           c book

**4** Complete the conversation with the words in the box.

> nineteen   Germany   Italian   waitress
> backpack   student   girlfriend   later

**Max**  Who's that girl with Frank? Is she his sister?
**Sue**  No. That's his new [1]_____ .
**Max**  Wow! Is she from here?
**Sue**  No, she's from [2]_____ .
**Max**  She's beautiful. How old is she?
**Sue**  She's [3]_____ .
**Max**  Is she a college [4]_____ ?
**Sue**  No, she's a [5]_____ at the [6]_____ restaurant on Green Street.
**Max**  Oh no, I'm late for class. See you [7]_____ .
**Sue**  Hey ... is that your [8]_____ ?
**Max**  Yes, it is. Thanks!
**Sue**  Bye.

# Personal Best

**Lesson Hello**
Write a phrase to introduce a friend to someone.

**Lesson 2A**
Name four items in your purse or backpack.

**Lesson 1A**
Name five nationalities, but not your own.

**Lesson 2A**
Describe one of your personal items.

**Lesson 1B**
Describe someone, including their job and nationality.

**Lesson 2B**
Write two of your favorite colors.

**Lesson 1B**
Write three questions to ask a new student in your class.

**Lesson 2B**
Describe something in the classroom.

**Lesson 1C**
Write the ages of three people in your family.

**Lesson 2C**
Write two sentences about people in your family.

**Lesson 1D**
Write three words that always start with capital letters.

**Lesson 2D**
Write what time it is now.

# Food and drink

| LANGUAGE | simple present (*I, you, we, they*) ■ food and drink |
|---|---|

## 3A Food for athletes

**1** ▶ **3.1** Put the words in the box in the correct columns. Listen and check.

eggs   orange juice   meat   tea   coffee   bread   rice   water

| We eat ... | We drink ... |
|---|---|
|  |  |

Personal Best

Go to Vocabulary practice: food and drink, page 112

**2** In pairs, talk about food and drink that you like and don't like.

☺ *I like meat.*      ☹ *I don't like coffee.*

**3** **A** Look at the pictures. What food can you see? Is it healthy?

**B** Match pictures a and b with the athletes. Read the text quickly and check.

# Olympic Diets   What do Olympic athletes eat for breakfast, lunch, and dinner? We talk to two very different athletes.

a

b

## Artem Petrenko, Weightlifter, Ukraine

**What do you have for breakfast?**
For breakfast, I eat six eggs and three or four cheese sandwiches. I drink a liter of orange juice and three cups of coffee.

**What about lunch and dinner?**
I have lunch at 1:00 p.m. I eat a big bowl of pasta or rice, and salad. For dinner, I eat meat – with potatoes and vegetables. During the day, I eat more sandwiches and fruit.

**That's a lot of food! What's your favorite food?**
Cheese. I love all cheese, and my favorite is Dutch cheese, like Gouda.

## Michelle Nelson, Marathon runner, Australia

**What do you have for breakfast?**
For breakfast, I eat whole wheat bread and fruit, and I drink "green juice" – it's juice with green vegetables and fruit. I'm a vegan, so I don't eat meat, eggs, or fish, and I don't drink milk.

**What about lunch and dinner?**
For lunch, I have a vegan burger with rice and salad. In the evening, I have dinner with my family. It's difficult because we don't like the same things! But we all eat pizza. My two sisters like cheese, but I have a vegan pizza – without cheese!

**Do marathon runners eat dessert?**
Yes, they do! Well, maybe not all of them ... but I love dessert. It's my favorite part of the meal. I love carrot cake and vegan ice cream.

**4** Read the text again and complete the sentences with the correct words.

1 What _____ you _____ for breakfast?
2 I _____ a liter of orange juice.
3 I _____ lunch at 1:00 p.m.
4 I _____ milk.
5 We _____ the same things.
6 _____ marathon runners _____ dessert?

**5** **A** Look at the sentences in exercise 4 and answer the questions.

1 Which sentences are affirmative?  _____ and _____
2 Which are negative?  _____ and _____
3 Which are questions?  _____ and _____

**B** Complete the rules. Then read the Grammar box.

1 We use _____ + verb in negative simple present sentences with *I, you, we,* and *they*.
2 We use _____ + subject + verb in simple present questions with *I, you, we,* and *they*.

> 📖 **Grammar**    **simple present (*I, you, we, they*)**
>
> **Affirmative:**
> *I **drink** a lot of water.*
> *We **eat** ice cream for dessert.*
>
> **Negative:**
> *You **don't drink** coffee.*
> *They **don't like** vegetables.*
>
> **Questions and short answers:**
> ***Do** you **like** fish?*
> *Yes, I **do**.    No, I **don't**.*

**Go to Grammar practice:** simple present (*I, you, we, they*), page 98

**6** ▶3.4 **Pronunciation:** *do you* /dəyuw/ Listen and repeat the questions. Pay attention to the pronunciation of *do you* /dəyuw/.

1 Do you like pizza?    2 What do you eat for breakfast?    3 What food do you like?

**7** **A** ▶3.5 Say the questions. Listen, check, and repeat.

1 Do you like Mexican food?
2 Do you eat meat?
3 Do you drink tea?
4 Do you like chocolate?
5 What time do you have breakfast?
6 What do you have for lunch?

**B** Ask and answer the questions in pairs.

**8** **A** ▶3.6 Complete the text with the verbs in parentheses. Listen and check.

## Comfort food

What food [1]_____ (you / like) after a hard day? What
[2]_____ (you / eat) when you're sad? What's your "comfort food"?

I'm a student. After a hard day at school,
[3]_____
(we / always have) ice cream.
[4]_____ (I / like)
caramel – it's my favorite!

**Harriet, the U.S.**

My children are strange.
[5]_____
(they / not like) regular sandwiches.
[6]_____ (they / eat)
banana and cheese sandwiches!

**Mike, Canada**

I'm a doctor. When I'm tired or sad, [7]_____
(I / not eat) chocolate or pizza – it's bad for you. [8]_____
(I / drink) green tea.

**Rosa, Argentina**

**B** In pairs, talk about your "comfort food." What do you eat or drink when you're sad or tired?

**Go to Communication practice:** Student A page 136, Student B page 144

**9** **A** Ask and answer questions in pairs.

1 like / Japanese food
2 drink / a lot of soda
3 have / dinner with your family
4 eat / a lot of fruit
5 drink / coffee at night
6 eat / a lot of red meat

**A** *Do you like Japanese food?*    **B** *No, I don't. But I like Chinese food.*

**B** Tell the class what you and your partner have in common.

*We don't like Japanese food, but we like Chinese food.*

**Personal Best** Write what you have for breakfast, lunch, and dinner on a typical day.

Learning Curve

## 3B Tea or coffee?

**1** Complete the café sign with the days of the week.

Friday   Tuesday   Wednesday   Sunday

**Riverside Café**

We are open:

| Monday | Closed |
|---|---|
| 1 _____ | 9:00 a.m. – 5:00 p.m. |
| 2 _____ | 9:00 a.m. – 5:00 p.m. |
| Thursday | Closed |
| 3 _____ | 9:00 a.m. – 9:00 p.m. |
| Saturday | 10:00 a.m. – 11:00 p.m. |
| 4 _____ | 10:00 a.m. – 4:00 p.m. |

Hot food & sandwiches!
Coffee & cake!

Personal Best

**Go to Vocabulary practice:** days and times of day, page 116

**2** Look at the sign in exercise 1 again. Are the sentences true (T) or false (F)?

1 The café is open every day. _____
2 It's open in the morning on Tuesdays. _____
3 It's open on Thursday afternoons. _____
4 It's open in the evening on Fridays. _____
5 It's closed on Saturday nights. _____
6 It's closed in the evening on Sundays. _____

**3** Ask and answer the questions in pairs.

1 What day is it today?
2 What day is it tomorrow?
3 What day was it yesterday?
4 What's your favorite day of the week?
5 What's the worst day of the week?
6 What's your favorite time of day?

**4** **A** ▶3.8  Watch or listen to the first part of the show. Check (✔) the sentence which is correct.

1 People drink coffee in cafés and tea at home. ☐
2 People drink tea and coffee all over the world. ☐
3 People drink coffee in the morning and tea in the evening. ☐

**B** ▶3.8  Watch or listen again. Match the parts to make sentences.

Learning Curve

1 54% of Americans
2 65% of those people
3 35% of those people
4 In the UK, people drink 165 million
5 In the UK, people drink 70 million

a cups of tea every day.
b drink coffee at lunch or later.
c drink coffee every day.
d drink coffee in the morning.
e cups of coffee every day.

**5** ▶ 3.9   Watch or listen to the second part of the show. Match the people with the food and drink.

 Jolene    Ioan    Chan    Ethan    Kate

1 fish, rice, vegetables, tea, water _____
2 cookies, ice cream, coffee _____
3 fish and chips and tea _____

4 sandwich, chips, cookie, tea _____
5 coffee, cereal _____

🔧 **Skill**   **listening for times and days**

Listen carefully when people talk about times and days.
- Times and days can come at the beginning or end of a sentence: *On Friday, I go to the café. / I go to the café on Friday.*
- Some times and days sound similar: *It's three fifteen. / It's three fifty.   Today is Tuesday. / Today is Thursday.*

**6** ▶ 3.9   Read the Skill box. Watch or listen again, and choose the correct options to complete the sentences.

1 **Kate:**   It's *2:30 p.m. / 2:40 p.m.* here, and I'm with Jolene.
2 **Jolene:**   We come here every *Tuesday / Thursday*. It's my husband's favorite café.
3 **Jolene:**   I drink coffee every *morning / evening*, but between 2:30 and *3:00 / 3:30*, I drink tea.
4 **Ioan:**   The party's at *8:00 p.m. / 9:00 p.m.*
5 **Chan:**   We're open *Monday / Sunday* through Friday from 11:00 a.m. until 10:00 p.m. And Saturday and Sunday from 10:00 a.m. until *7:00 p.m. / 11:00 p.m.*
6 **Kate:**   It's *3:15 / 3:30* here, and I have fish and chips from my favorite takeaway place!

**7**   In pairs, talk about what food and drink you have every day.

*I have a coffee at 10:00 in the morning.*

**8** ▶ 3.10   Listen to the extract from the show. How does Ethan pronounce *and*?

> I have a coffee **and** cereal.

🧩 **Listening builder**   /ə/

The /ə/ sound is also called "schwa." It is very common in English in short unstressed words, like articles, prepositions, and auxiliary verbs.

| /ə/ /ə/ | /ə/ | /ə/ | /ə/ |
|---|---|---|---|
| a cup of tea | We have coffee at 9:00 p.m. | What time's the party? | Does she like fish? |

**9** ▶ 3.11   Read the Listening builder. Then listen and complete the sentences.

1 I have _____ coffee every morning.
2 What _____ they eat?
3 They only drink coffee _____ breakfast.
4 This one's _____ you.
5 I have two bottles _____ water.
6 I like burgers _____ French fries.

**10**   Think of a café that you like. In pairs, ask and answer the questions about the café.

What's its name?   Where is it?   When do you go there?

What do you eat or drink there?   What do other people have?   Why do you like it?

## 3C Chocolate for breakfast!

**1** Complete phrases 1–6 with the verbs in the box.

> use  watch  have  go  make  say

1 _____ "hello"  2 _____ a cat  3 _____ dinner  4 _____ running  5 _____ a computer  6 _____ TV

**Go to Vocabulary practice:** common verbs (1), page 113

**2** Ask and answer the questions in pairs.

1 you / live near downtown?
2 you / work in an office?
3 you / make dinner at home every evening?
4 you / know three languages?
5 you / say "hello" to a lot of people every day?
6 you / have brothers or sisters?

**3** ▶ 3.13  Look at the picture of Adam Young. What is his job? Read and listen to the text and check.

## THE BEST JOB IN THE WORLD?

From Monday through Friday, Adam Young eats chocolate at work. That's because Adam is a *chocolatier* (he makes chocolate). "I love it," he says. "I think it's a great job!" Adam lives in Brooklyn in New York. He has a small store, and he makes all of his chocolates by hand. Does he have the best job in the world? This is his typical day. "In the morning, I go to the store early and make chocolate ... I eat it for breakfast! Then we work here all day."

Adam has an assistant, Jenny. When he's in the kitchen with the chocolate, Jenny works with the customers.
Adam exercises a lot – very important when you eat chocolate all day! In the evening, he changes his clothes and goes to the gym. Then he goes home, makes dinner, and watches TV.
On the weekend, he studies business – he says it's important for his job ... but he doesn't eat chocolate!

**4 A** Choose the correct words to complete the sentences. What letter do we add to the verbs with *he, she,* and *it* in affirmative sentences?

1 Adam Young *eat / eats* chocolate at work.
2 He *make / makes* all of his chocolates by hand.
3 I go to the store early and *make / makes* chocolate.
4 I *eat / eats* it for breakfast!
5 Then we *work / works* here all day.
6 Jenny *work / works* with the customers.

**B** Find the *he/she/it* forms of the verbs in the text.

1 say _____
2 live _____
3 have _____
4 exercise _____
5 change _____
6 go _____
7 watch _____
8 study _____

**5** Find a question and a negative sentence in the text. Complete the rules, and then read the Grammar box.

   1 We use _____ + verb in negative simple present sentences with *he/she/it*.
   2 We use _____ + subject + verb in simple present questions with *he/she/it*.

📖 **Grammar**  **simple present (*he, she, it*)**

| **Affirmative:** | **Negative:** | **Questions and short answers:** |
| --- | --- | --- |
| She **eats** fruit for breakfast. | He **doesn't work** in a school. | **Does** your house **have** a yard? |
| He **watches** TV in the evening. | She **doesn't** exercise. | Yes, it **does**.   No, it **doesn't**. |
| Maya **studies** English. | My wife **doesn't like** chocolate. | |

**Look!** Some verbs are irregular: *do > does, go > goes, have > has*.

**Go to Grammar practice:** simple present (*he, she, it*), page 98

**6 A** ▶ 3.15  **Pronunciation:** *-s* and *-es* endings  Listen and repeat the sounds and words. Pay attention to the pronunciation of the *-s* and *-es* endings.

   1 /s/    eats    works    makes
   2 /z/    lives    goes    knows
   3 /ɪz/    watches    uses    changes

**B** ▶ 3.16  Match the parts to make sentences. Listen, check, and repeat.

| | | | |
| --- | --- | --- | --- |
| 1 | She lives | a | movies in the afternoon. |
| 2 | He works | b | in an office. |
| 3 | She watches | c | a computer at work. |
| 4 | He says | d | "Hi" every day. |
| 5 | She makes | e | in Tokyo. |
| 6 | He uses | f | cakes on the weekend. |

**7** ▶ 3.17  Complete the text with the correct form of the verbs in the box. Listen and check.

> have   exercise   eat   say   work   make   go

## A VERY COOL JOB

Kirsten Lind [1]_____ for an ice cream company in Toronto. She [2]_____ a great job – she's a food scientist, and she [3]_____ new flavors of ice cream. What's this week's new flavor? "Potato chips and chocolate! I don't like potato chips, but lots of people love it," Kirsten [4]_____ . Kirsten [5]_____ two or three liters of ice cream a week, so she [6]_____ to the gym after work, and she [7]_____ a lot on the weekend.

**8 A** Make questions about the text in exercise 7.

   1 Kirsten / work / in a store?         _____
   2 she / have / an interesting job?     _____
   3 she / eat / a lot of potato chips?   _____
   4 she / exercise / a lot?              _____

**B** Ask and answer the questions in pairs. Use short answers.

**Go to Communication practice:** Student A page 136, Student B page 144

**9** Choose three friends or family members and write down their names. Ask and answer the questions in pairs.

   **A** *Who is Ivan?*          **B** *He's my uncle.*
   **A** *Where does he live?*   **B** *He lives in ...*

   Who is … ?   Where does he/she live?   Where does he/she work?

   Does he/she like his/her job?   What does he/she do on the weekend?

## 3D A special meal

**1** **A** Match the food in the box with the celebrations in the pictures. What do you know about these celebration◄

> pancakes   chow mein   turkey   candy

Thanksgiving, U.S.

Carnevale, Italy

Chinese New Year, China

Maslenitsa, Russia

**B** Think of some important celebrations and festivals in your country. What do people eat and drink?

**2** Look at the pictures in Arusha's blog. What country is she from? How do people celebrate this festival? Read the text quickly and check.

# Arusha's Blog

MY POSTS | CONTACT ME | SEARCH

**About me**

Hi! I'm Arusha, I'm 25, and I live in Kerala in India. Welcome to my blog!

### Festival time

We have lots of festivals in India, and my favorite is Onam.

In the afternoon, we have a big meal with lots of food – some people have 24 dishes or more. We eat curry, rice, vegetables, and fruit, but we don't eat meat. We eat the food on a big banana leaf.

It's traditional to have lunch at home, but these days some people go to restaurants. In my family, we eat at my brother's house. After the meal, we meet friends, we listen to music, and we watch the tiger dance. What's my favorite thing about Onam? It's a really happy time, and the food is great.

**3** Read the text again and answer the questions.

1 What is the name of the festival?
2 When do people have the meal?
3 What food does Arusha eat?

4 What doesn't she eat?
5 Where does she have lunch?
6 What does she do after the meal?

**4** Read the Skill box. Find an example of each type of punctuation in the text on page 30.

> 🔧 **Skill** | **punctuation**
>
> It's important to use the correct punctuation to help people understand your writing.
>
> | . | **period:** | We use this at the end of a sentence. |
> |---|---|---|
> | , | **comma:** | We use this to separate ideas and after times. |
> | ? | **question mark:** | We use this at the end of a question. |
> | ' | **apostrophe:** | We use this in contractions and in *'s* for possession. |
> | A | **capital letters:** | (see the Text builder on page 13) |

**5** Rewrite the text about Chinese New Year with the correct punctuation and capital letters.

## whats your favorite festival

my names wu and im from nanjing in china my favorite festival is chinese new year its a national holiday and people dont work we have a big party with all the family and in the evening we eat meat fish rice and vegetables my mother makes a special cake and we give money to the children in the family

**6** Choose the correct words to complete the sentences from Arusha's blog. Check your answers in the text.

1 We eat curry, rice, vegetables, and fruit, *and / but* we don't eat meat.
2 It's a really happy time, *and / but* the food is great.

> 🧩 **Text builder** | **linking words (*and*, *but*)**
>
> We use *and* and *but* to link sentences.
> **To add information:** *We dance **and** we listen to music.*
> **To contrast different ideas:** *Some people go to restaurants, **but** our family eats at home.*

**7** Read the Text builder. Complete the sentences with *and* or *but*.

1 We go to my grandmother's house every Sunday, _____ we have a big meal.
2 This restaurant is expensive, _____ the food isn't very good.
3 I drink tea and fruit juice, _____ I don't drink coffee.
4 Claire works in the morning, _____ she doesn't work in the afternoon.
5 My uncle lives in Los Angeles, _____ he's not American.
6 He exercises, _____ he goes to the gym.

**8 A** **PREPARE** Choose a festival or celebration in your country where food is important. Think about these questions.

- When is the festival or celebration?
- What do people eat and drink?
- Where do you eat and who do you eat with?
- What do you do before and after the meal?

**B** **PRACTICE** Write a blog about the festival or celebration. Link your sentences with *and* and *but*.

**C** **PERSONAL BEST** Exchange your blog with your partner. Check the grammar and punctuation. Are the simple present verbs correct? Does your partner use *and* and *but* correctly?

**Personal Best** Think of a special meal. Write three sentences about it with *and*, and three sentences with *but*.

# Daily life

## 4A Day and night

**1 A** ▶ 4.1 Match the phrases in the box with pictures a–e. Listen and check.

start work   finish work   go to bed   get home   get up

**B** In pairs, say what time you do the activities.

**A** *I get up at 6:30.*        **B** *That's early! I get up at 8:30.*

**Go to Vocabulary practice:** daily routine verbs, page 114

**Personal Best**

**2** Look at the pictures and guess the answers to the questions. Read the text and check.

1 What is the relationship between the two people?
2 What are their jobs?
3 Are their routines similar or different?

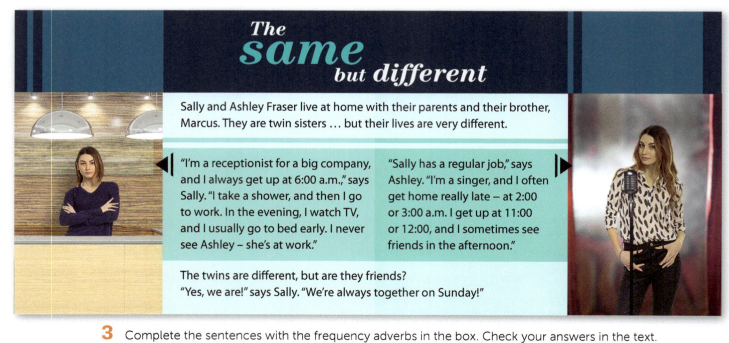

## The same but different

Sally and Ashley Fraser live at home with their parents and their brother, Marcus. They are twin sisters … but their lives are very different.

"I'm a receptionist for a big company, and I always get up at 6:00 a.m.," says Sally. "I take a shower, and then I go to work. In the evening, I watch TV, and I usually go to bed early. I never see Ashley – she's at work."

"Sally has a regular job," says Ashley. "I'm a singer, and I often get home really late – at 2:00 or 3:00 a.m. I get up at 11:00 or 12:00, and I sometimes see friends in the afternoon."

The twins are different, but are they friends?
"Yes, we are!" says Sally. "We're always together on Sunday!"

**3** Complete the sentences with the frequency adverbs in the box. Check your answers in the text.

always   sometimes   usually   never   often

1 I _____ see Ashley.
2 I _____ see friends in the afternoon.
3 I _____ get home really late.
4 I _____ go to bed early.
5 I _____ get up at 6:00 a.m.

**4** **A** Put the frequency adverbs in the box in the correct order.

> sometimes   usually   never

100% ──────────────────────────────────────────────── 0%

always     1 _____     often     2 _____     3 _____

**B** Read the sentences in exercise 3 again. Do the frequency adverbs come before or after the verbs? Read the Grammar box.

---

📖 **Grammar** **frequency adverbs**

100%
**always:** I **always** have breakfast at home.
**usually:** She **usually** takes a shower in the morning.
**often:** I **often** get up late on the weekend.
**sometimes:** I **sometimes** get home at 1:00 a.m.
0% **never:** She **never** has dinner at home.

**Look!** Frequency adverbs come after the verb *be*: We're **always** together on Sunday.

---

**Go to Grammar practice:** frequency adverbs, page 99

**5** **A** ▶4.4 **Pronunciation:** sentence stress  Listen to the sentences. Are the frequency adverbs stressed or unstressed?

1 I usually get up at 7:00 a.m.
2 I always have a cup of coffee for breakfast.

3 I never go to the gym.
4 I often make dinner in the evening.

**B** Listen again, check, and repeat.

**6** Change the frequency adverbs in 5A so the sentences are true for you.
In pairs, say the sentences with the correct stress.
**A** *I sometimes get up at 7:00 a.m.*      **B** *Really? I never get up at 7:00 a.m.*

**7** **A** Look at the chart. Write five sentences about Sally and Ashley's brother, Marcus.
*He always has breakfast in a café.*

| | Mon | Tue | Wed | Thu | Fri |
|---|---|---|---|---|---|
| 1 have breakfast in a café | ✔ | ✔ | ✔ | ✔ | ✔ |
| 2 watch TV in the morning | ✔ | ✘ | ✔ | ✘ | ✔ |
| 3 work in the evening | ✔ | ✘ | ✔ | ✔ | ✔ |
| 4 see friends after work | ✘ | ✘ | ✘ | ✘ | ✔ |
| 5 go to bed before midnight | ✘ | ✘ | ✘ | ✘ | ✘ |

**B** ▶4.5 Listen and check. What is Marcus's job?

**Go to Communication practice:** Student A page 136, Student B page 144

**8** In pairs, compare yourself with members of your family. Use the activities in the boxes.
*I always get up before 7:00 a.m., but my brother usually gets up late, at 9:30.*

> get up before 7:00 a.m.   eat fast food   watch TV in the morning   go to bed late

> get home before 6:00 p.m.   have coffee for breakfast   have lunch at work   take a shower in the morning

---

## 4B My trip to work

**1** Match the types of transportation with pictures a−e on page 35.

1 bike _____
2 taxi _____
3 bus _____
4 car _____
5 subway _____

**Go to Vocabulary practice:** transportation, page 115

**2** Look at the pictures and the title of the text on page 35. Guess the answers to the questions. Read the text quickly and check.

1 What city is it about?
2 What type of transportation is it about?

---

**Skill** | finding specific information

**We sometimes need to find specific information in a text.**
- Read the questions carefully to see what information you need to find.
- Find the place in the text which has this information and read it carefully.
- Don't worry if you don't understand every word.

---

**3 A** Read the Skill box. Then find information in the paragraph about Emily in the text to complete the first line of the chart.

|  | Lives where? | Which job? | Works where? |
|---|---|---|---|
| Emily | *Harlem* |  |  |
| Dan |  |  |  |
| Megan |  |  |  |
| Walter |  |  |  |

**B** Now find the information about the other people in the text. Complete the chart.

**4** Read the text again. Then, in pairs, say why each person uses a *citibike*.

*Emily uses a citibike because it's fast.*

**5** Complete the sentences from the text. In which sentences does 's mean *is*?

1 _____ office is in Downtown Manhattan.
2 "The _____ cheap," she says.

---

**Text builder** | 's: possession or contraction

If you see 's at the end of a word, decide if it refers to possession or if it is a contraction of *is*.
The **city's** blue public bikes = **possession** (the bikes belong to the city)
**Megan's** a waitress on the Lower East Side = **contraction** (Megan is a waitress)

---

**6** Read the Text builder. Then read the sentences and write *P* (possession) or *C* (contraction).

1 Ravi's a doctor. _____
2 David's mom is a teacher. _____
3 My train's always late. _____
4 Julia's brother starts work at 7:00. _____

**7** Discuss the questions in pairs.

1 Do you have public bikes in your town or city? Are they popular? Why/Why not?
2 How do you usually travel to work or school?
3 Do you like the trip? Why/Why not?

# A morning in the life of bike 0827

New York is famous for its yellow taxis and noisy subway, but a lot of people also travel by *citibike* – the city's blue public bikes. New Yorkers make 14 million trips a year on *citibikes*. Who uses them and why? We follow one bike for a morning to find out.

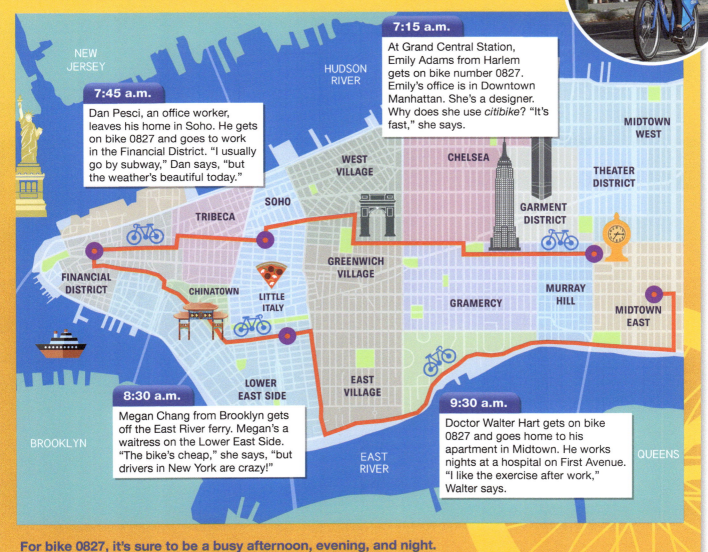

**7:15 a.m.**
At Grand Central Station, Emily Adams from Harlem gets on bike number 0827. Emily's office is in Downtown Manhattan. She's a designer. Why does she use *citibike*? "It's fast," she says.

**7:45 a.m.**
Dan Pesci, an office worker, leaves his home in Soho. He gets on bike 0827 and goes to work in the Financial District. "I usually go by subway," Dan says, "but the weather's beautiful today."

**8:30 a.m.**
Megan Chang from Brooklyn gets off the East River ferry. Megan's a waitress on the Lower East Side. "The bike's cheap," she says, "but drivers in New York are crazy!"

**9:30 a.m.**
Doctor Walter Hart gets on bike 0827 and goes home to his apartment in Midtown. He works nights at a hospital on First Avenue. "I like the exercise after work," Walter says.

For bike 0827, it's sure to be a busy afternoon, evening, and night.

**Personal Best**   Write about the different types of transportation in your town or city.

## 4C Where do you work?

**1** Match the adjectives in the box with their opposites.

> quiet   clean   hot   fast   unfriendly

1 dirty / _____   2 cold / _____   3 friendly / _____   4 noisy / _____   5 slow / _____

**Go to Vocabulary practice:** adjectives (2), page 116

**2 A** Write down two examples for each of these things.

> a cold country   a large building in your country   a noisy job   a long river   a fast animal
>
> a friendly café or store in your town or city   a hot drink   a quiet place in your town or city

**B** Compare your answers in pairs. Do you have the same things?

**3** Read the text quickly and answer the questions.

1 What is Tess's job?   _____   3 What time does she start work?   _____
2 Does she like her job?   _____   4 Where does she live?   _____

# A Dirty Job?

 Tess Mitchell is a garbage collector. It's dirty work, and she gets up very early, but she loves her job.

**What time do you start work?**
I start work at 5:00 in the morning. I get up at 4:15 a.m. and have breakfast. Then I leave for work.

**¹_____ do you work?**
I work in south Chicago. The landfill isn't far from my house.

**²_____ do you do on a typical day?**
I drive the truck to about 800 houses every day from Monday through Friday. That's a lot of trash!

**³_____ do you like the job?**
Because the people are friendly and I work outside. Sometimes it's very cold early in the morning, but when the weather's nice, I love it.

**⁴_____ do you finish work?**
I finish at 1:30 p.m. I'm a mom, so the hours are great. I get home at 2:00, take a shower, and then I go to my children's school to pick them up.

**⁵_____ do you relax when you're not at work?**
I play soccer with a women's soccer team, and we practice on Tuesday and Thursday evenings. On the weekend, I get up late!

**4 A** Complete the questions in the text with the question words in the box. How do you say them in your language?

> Why   Where   When   What   How

**B** Look at the questions in the text again. Order the words below from 1–4 to make a question. Then read the Grammar box.

☐ *do/does*    ☐ main verb    ☐ question word    ☐ subject

| Grammar | simple present: *wh-* questions |
| --- | --- |

| Question word: | *do/does*: | Subject: | Main verb: |
| --- | --- | --- | --- |
| *Where* | *do* | *you* | *live?* |
| *What* | *does* | *your husband* | *do?* |
| *How* | *does* | *he* | *get to work?* |
| *When* | *do* | *your children* | *watch TV?* |
| *What time* | *do* | *they* | *get up?* |
| *Why* | *do* | *you* | *work on the weekend?* |
| *Who* | *do* | *you* | *work with?* |

**Go to Grammar practice:** simple present: *wh-* questions, page 99

**5** ▶ 4.10   **Pronunciation:** question words   Listen and repeat the question words. Do they begin with a /w/ sound or a /h/ sound?

1 where _____   2 when _____   3 who _____   4 why _____   5 how _____   6 what _____

**6 A** ▶ 4.11   Order the words to make questions. Say the questions with the correct pronunciation of the question words. Listen, check, and repeat.

1 you / have / how many / do / children   _____ ?
2 what / they / time / have breakfast / do   _____ ?
3 do / does / husband / your / what   _____ ?
4 he / when / does / work   _____ ?
5 on the weekend / you / what / do / do   _____ ?

**B** ▶ 4.12   Match questions 1–5 with answers a–e. Listen to the interview with Tess and check.

a  In the afternoons and evenings.
b  Two.
c  He's a taxi driver.
d  7:30.
e  We often go to the park.

**Go to Communication practice:** Student A page 137, Student B page 145

**7 A** Find out about your partner. Ask and answer the questions in the boxes in pairs.

> What time / start work?   Who / live with?   How / get to your English classes?

> What / have for breakfast?   Where / usually go on vacation?   How / relax in the evening?

> Why / study English?   When / do your English homework?   How many brothers and sisters / have?

**B** Switch partners. Ask and answer questions about your first partner.

**A** *What time does Sasha start work?*    **B** *He usually starts work at 8:00 a.m.*

 Write ten questions for an interview with an actor/singer that you like.

## 4D How can I help you?

**1 A** ▶ 4.13 Match the prices with the words. Listen and check.

a £5  b $50  c €15  d £5.95  e 50p  f 50c

g $19.99  h $9.99  i $25  j $11.99  k $6.50  l $29

| | | |
|---|---|---|
| 1 nine dollars ninety-nine | _____ | |
| 2 nineteen dollars ninety-nine | _____ | |
| 3 fifteen euros | _____ | |
| 4 fifty dollars | _____ | |
| 5 eleven dollars ninety-nine | _____ | |
| 6 twenty-nine dollars | _____ | |

| | |
|---|---|
| 7 fifty pence | _____ |
| 8 five pounds | _____ |
| 9 six dollars fifty | _____ |
| 10 fifty cents | _____ |
| 11 five pounds ninety-five | _____ |
| 12 twenty-five dollars | _____ |

**B** Write down three prices in numbers and give them to your partner. Say your partner's prices.

*That's three dollars fifty.*

**2** Discuss the questions in pairs.

1 Who usually goes grocery shopping in your house?
2 Where do you usually buy groceries? Why?
   **a** at a supermarket   **b** at a market   **c** at local stores
3 Do you like grocery shopping? Why/Why not?

Penny

**3** ▶ 4.14 Watch or listen to the first part of *Learning Curve*. Are the sentences true (T) or false (F)?

1 Penny likes grocery shopping. _____
2 Penny and Taylor live together. _____
3 They usually go grocery shopping on Thursdays. _____
4 There is a big supermarket near their apartment. _____

**4** ▶ 4.15 Watch or listen to the second part of the show. Check (✔) the things Penny buys and the correct prices.

| store 1 | | store 2 | | store 3 | |
|---|---|---|---|---|---|
| half a chicken | ☐ | cheese and salad | ☐ | a blue shopping cart | ☐ |
| a whole chicken | ☐ | cheese and eggs | ☐ | a black shopping cart | ☐ |
| $4.79 | ☐ | $17.15 | ☐ | $21.77 | ☐ |
| $8.79 | ☐ | $17.50 | ☐ | $22.02 | ☐ |

**5** ▶ 4.15 Who says the phrases: Penny (P), Salesclerk 1 (S1), Salesclerk 2 (S2), or Salesclerk 3 (S3)? Watch or listen again, and check.

1 How much is it for that small shopping cart? _____
2 Here you go. _____
3 I'd like a whole chicken, please. _____
4 You're welcome. _____
5 Here's your change – 25 cents. _____
6 Can I have two pounds of this white cheese? _____

## Conversation builder   grocery shopping

**Customer:**

*Do you have ...?*   *How much is that?*

*Can I have ...*   *Here you go/are.*

*I'd like ...*

**Salesclerk:**

*How can I help you?*   *Here you are.*

*Anything else?*   *Here's your change.*

*That's ... dollars.*   *Have a nice day!*

**6  A** Read the Conversation builder. Then, order the sentences from 1–7 to make a conversation in a store.

**a** ☐ Yes. Anything else?

**b** ☐ Yes, I'd like five cookies, please. How much is that?

**c** ☐ Can I have a chocolate cake, please?

**d** ☐ Thanks. And here's your change.

**e** ☐ Here you are – $10.

**f** ☐ Hello. How can I help you?

**g** ☐ That's $8.50.

**B** ▶ 4.16  Listen and check. Practice the conversation in pairs.

**7** ▶ 4.17  Complete the conversation with the words in the box. Listen and check. Are Penny and the salesclerk polite? Why/Why not?

welcome   good   thank you   please

**Salesclerk**  ¹_____ evening.

**Penny**  I'd like a whole chicken, ²_____ .

**Salesclerk**  Here you are.

**Penny**  ³_____ .

**Salesclerk**  You're ⁴_____ .

## 🔧 Skill   being polite in stores

**It's important to be polite if you work in a store or if you're a customer.**

- Greet people. Say: *Hi / Good morning / Good evening*, etc.
- Ask for things politely. Say: *Can I have ...? / I'd like ..., please.* NOT ~~I want ... / Give me ...~~
- If someone says: *Thanks / Thank you*, you can reply: *You're welcome.*
- Salesclerks often end by saying: *Have a nice day!*

**8** ▶ 4.18  Read the Skill box. Listen to three conversations. Check (✔) the people who are polite.

**1 a** the customer ☐   **b** the waiter ☐   **c** both people ☐

**2 a** the customer ☐   **b** the salesclerk ☐   **c** both people ☐

**3 a** the customer ☐   **b** the receptionist ☐   **c** both people ☐

**Go to Communication practice:** Student A page 137, Student B page 145

**9  A** PREPARE  In pairs, look at the pictures and choose one of the situations. Write down things you can buy there and their prices.

In a restaurant

At a market

In a café

**B** PRACTICE  Decide who is the customer and who is the salesclerk. Act out your conversation.

**C** PERSONAL BEST  Listen to another pair's conversation. Are they polite? What could they do better?

**Personal Best**   Think of your favorite grocery store or café and write a conversation in English there.

# Grammar

**1**   Check (✔) the correct sentences.

1   a   I never finish work at 5:00 p.m. ☐
    b   I don't never finish work at 5:00 p.m. ☐
    c   I don't finish work never at 5:00 p.m. ☐

2   a   He don't go to bed early. ☐
    b   He not go to bed early. ☐
    c   He doesn't go to bed early. ☐

3   a   Do you go to work by car? ☐
    b   Does you go to work by car? ☐
    c   When you do go to work by car? ☐

4   a   We often has eggs for breakfast. ☐
    b   We often have eggs for breakfast. ☐
    c   We have often eggs for breakfast. ☐

5   a   Why do you live with? ☐
    b   Who do you live with? ☐
    c   How do you live with? ☐

6   a   When they do get up? ☐
    b   When they get up? ☐
    c   When do they get up? ☐

7   a   She work in a restaurant in the evening. ☐
    b   She do work in a restaurant in the evening. ☐
    c   She works in a restaurant in the evening. ☐

8   a   Goes he to the gym after work? ☐
    b   Does he to the gym after work? ☐
    c   Does he go to the gym after work? ☐

**2**   Order the words to make questions and sentences.

1   your / do / go / children / where / school / to

    _____ ?

2   have / she / at / does / lunch / home

    _____ ?

3   always / dinner / we / eat / vegetables / for

    _____ .

4   get / time / what / weekend / do / up / the / you / on

    _____ ?

5   don't / shopping / I / Saturdays / go / on

    _____ .

6   the / he / book / sometimes / a / reads / train / on

    _____ .

7   Mondays / quiet / restaurant / is / on / often / the

    _____ .

8   in / radio / do / listen / to / you / the / morning / the

    _____ ?

9   old / brother's / is / how / your / girlfriend

    _____ ?

10   the / never / exercises / Simon / weekend / on

    _____ .

**3**   Complete the text with the correct form of the verbs in parentheses.

## Life on Muck

 This is Laura Marriner. She lives and works on the very small island of Muck in Scotland. Life isn't easy, but it's very interesting …

**What** ^1_____ (be) **Laura's job?**
She's a teacher. Her school only ^2_____ (have) eight children.

**Where** ^3_____ **she** _____ (live)?
Laura ^4 _____ (not leave) home in the morning because she lives in the school with her husband and two sons!

**How** ^5_____ **they** _____ (go) **shopping?**
By ferry. The trip is two hours, but people on the island only ^6_____ (use) the ferry when the weather is good. They ^7_____ (not go) shopping every day, so Laura ^8_____ (make) bread at home.

**What is school life like on Muck?**
It's great. The children often ^9_____ (study) on the beach.

^10_____ **Laura** _____ (like) **life on Muck?**
Yes, she does! When the weather is bad, life is difficult, but she's happy there. The people are very friendly, and life is an adventure.

# Vocabulary

**1**   Put the words in the box in the correct columns.

| ~~boat~~   ~~cold~~   do   cheese   fast   finish   get up |
| know   small   meat   noisy   short   taxi   train   want |

| Verbs | Adjectives | Nouns |
|-------|------------|-------|
| *do* | *cold* | *boat* |
|  |  |  |
|  |  |  |
|  |  |  |

**2** (Circle) the word that is different. Explain your answers.

| | | | |
|---|---|---|---|
| 1 | car | truck | bus | plane |
| 2 | think | use | slow | make |
| 3 | Friday | tomorrow | Sunday | Saturday |
| 4 | rice | French fries | potato chips | potatoes |
| 5 | coffee | milk | fruit | orange juice |
| 6 | clean | horrible | unfriendly | dirty |
| 7 | cookie | pizza | cake | chocolate |
| 8 | work | study | change | dinner |

**3** Complete the sentences with the correct words.

1 What time do you g_et_ home after work?

2 He usually l_____ to the radio at work.

3 I always have b_____ before I leave home in the morning.

4 They w_____ television after dinner.

5 She goes to school by m_____ . It's very fast.

6 In cold weather, I have a h_____ drink in the evening.

7 He never says "hello." He's so u_____ .

8 T_____ in New York are yellow, and in London they're black.

9 I never drink tea or coffee. I only drink w_____ with meals.

10 On W_____ evenings, I go to the gym.

**4** Complete the e-mail with the words in the box.

> bike   dressed   bread   friendly   get   live
> go   evening   Saturday   read

Hi Ana,

How are you? I'm in Cartagena at my grandmother's house this week. It's nice and quiet here. I ¹_____ up late every day, have breakfast, and get ²_____ . Then I go to the shopping mall by ³_____ . I usually buy some ⁴_____ for lunch. The people are very ⁵_____ . In the afternoon, I ⁶_____ to the beach and ⁷_____ a book. In the ⁸_____ , we sometimes have dinner in a restaurant.

I'm here for one week, and then I go home on ⁹_____ ☹ … I want to ¹⁰_____ here!

See you soon.

Bea

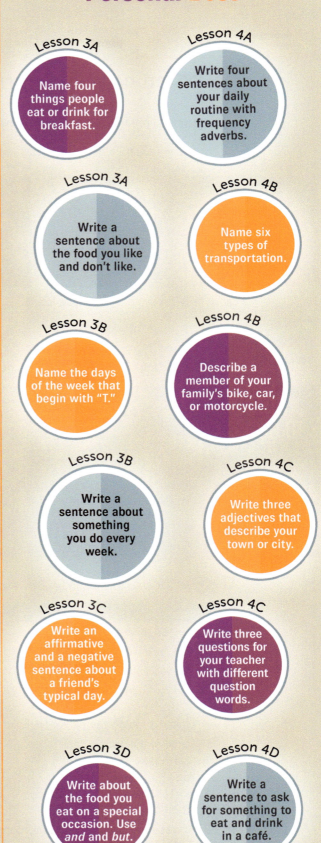

## Personal Best

**Lesson 3A**
Name four things people eat or drink for breakfast.

**Lesson 4A**
Write four sentences about your daily routine with frequency adverbs.

**Lesson 3A**
Write a sentence about the food you like and don't like.

**Lesson 4B**
Name six types of transportation.

**Lesson 3B**
Name the days of the week that begin with "T."

**Lesson 4B**
Describe a member of your family's bike, car, or motorcycle.

**Lesson 3B**
Write a sentence about something you do every week.

**Lesson 4C**
Write three adjectives that describe your town or city.

**Lesson 3C**
Write an affirmative and a negative sentence about a friend's typical day.

**Lesson 4C**
Write three questions for your teacher with different question words.

**Lesson 3D**
Write about the food you eat on a special occasion. Use *and* and *but*.

**Lesson 4D**
Write a sentence to ask for something to eat and drink in a café.

# All about me

## 5A When can you start?

**1** Complete phrases 1–5 with the verbs in the box.

swim  speak  drive  play  call

**1** _____ a car
**2** _____ Chinese
**3** _____ the piano
**4** _____ a friend
**5** _____ in the ocean

Go to Vocabulary practice: common verbs (2), page 117

**2** Read the job posting. What do you need for this job?

**JOBS TO GO.COM**
▸ FIND JOBS
▸ POST RÉSUMÉ
▸ COMPANY PROFILES

### SYDNEY CITY TOURS: TOUR GUIDE

Help tourists see the beautiful city of Sydney.

Do you know Sydney? Do you like working with people? Can you speak a foreign language? Do you want to work this summer?

If the answer is "Yes," then contact us.

▸ CONTACT

**3** ▶5.2 Listen to a job interview. Check (✔) the things Georgia can do. Does she get the job?

| | Yes | No |
|---|---|---|
| **1** Can you speak a foreign language? | | |
| **2** Can you drive? | | |
| **3** Can you work early in the morning? | | |
| **4** Can you swim well? | | |

**4 A** ▶5.2 Match the halves to make sentences. Listen again and check.

1 Some of the people can't          a can.
2 I can speak                        b start?
3 Yes, I                             c Chinese.
4 No, I                              d can't – sorry.
5 When can you                       e speak English.

**B** Choose the correct options to complete the rules. Then read the Grammar box.

1 We use *can* to talk about *abilities / daily routines*.
2 We use *can't* + verb in *questions / negatives*.
3 We use *can* + subject + verb in *questions / negatives*.

📖 **Grammar**   *can* and *can't*

| Affirmative: | Negative: | Questions and short answers: |
|---|---|---|
| I **can work** this summer. | I **can't speak** Chinese. | **Can** you **speak** a foreign language? |
| Georgia **can swim** well. | They **can't cook**. | Yes, I **can**.   No, I **can't**. |

Personal Best

**Go to Grammar practice:** *can* and *can't*, page 100

**5** ▶5.4  **Pronunciation:** *can* and *can't*  Listen and repeat. Pay attention to the difference between *can* /kæn/ or /kən/ and *can't* /kænt/.

1  He can drive.   2  She can't swim.   3  Can you play the guitar?   4  Yes, I can.

**6**  **A** ▶5.5  Say the sentences with the correct pronunciation of *can* and *can't*. Listen, check, and repeat.

1  I can swim two kilometers.   3  I can't speak German.   5  I can drive a car.
2  I can't sing well.   4  I can cook Italian food.   6  I can't play the piano.

**B**  Say the sentences in pairs. Say if you think it's true or false for your partner.

**A** *I can swim two kilometers.*   **B** *False. You can't swim two kilometers.*
**A** *You're right. I can't swim.*

**7**  **A**  Read the job posting. What does an *au pair* do?

**B** ▶5.6  Emily and Ben are interested in the job. Listen and check (✔) what they can and can't do.

### AU PAIR

- **Can you look after children?**
- **Do you like sports and music?**
- **Do you want to work as an au pair this summer?**

We're a friendly American family with two children. We live in Madrid, Spain.

– *Contact Lisa Jones for more information.* –

| Can he/she ... | Emily | Ben |
|---|---|---|
| cook? | | |
| drive? | | |
| speak Spanish? | | |
| play tennis? | | |
| swim? | | |
| play the piano? | | |
| play the guitar? | | |
| sing? | | |

**8** ▶5.7  In pairs, ask and answer the questions about Emily and Ben. Who is **best** for the job? Listen and check.

**A** *Can Emily cook?*   **B** *Yes, she can.*

**Go to Communication practice:** Student A page 137, Student B page 145

**9**  **A**  Ask your classmates questions 1–5. Find someone who says "Yes, I can." and write his/her name. Then ask for more information.

**A** *Can you speak a foreign language?*   **B** *Yes, I can.*
**A** *Which language can you speak?*   **B** *I can speak French.*

| Questions | Name | More information |
|---|---|---|
| 1  Can you speak a foreign language? | | |
| 2  Can you play an instrument? | | |
| 3  Can you dance? | | |
| 4  Can you cook? | | |
| 5  Can you play any sports? | | |

**B**  In pairs, discuss what you found out about your classmates.

*Sebastian can speak French.*

Personal **Best**   Write ten sentences about people in your class. Use *can* and *can't*.

## 5B I can't live without my phone

**1** Match the words in the box with the electronic devices 1–6. Is your family like this?

> headphones  laptop  smartphone  videogame  TV  remote control

1 _____  2 _____  3 _____  4 _____  5 _____  6 _____

**Go to Vocabulary practice:** electronic devices, page 118

**2** Which electronic devices do you have? Discuss in pairs.

*I have a laptop, but I don't have a tablet.*

**3** ▶5.9  Watch or listen to the first part of *Learning Curve*. Check (✔) the devices Kate mentions.

camera ☐   desktop computer ☐   TV ☐   smartphone ☐   laptop ☐   headphones ☐

🔧 **Skill**   listening for specific information

**We sometimes need to listen for specific information.**
- Read the questions to find out what information you need.
- Think about the topic and what type of information it is, e.g., a person, a place, or a number.
- Listen carefully when the speakers talk about this topic.

**4** ▶5.9  Read the Skill box. Watch or listen again, and choose the correct options to answer the questions.

1 Which sport does Kate play on Friday?
  **a** basketball   **b** soccer   **c** tennis
2 What language does she learn on her tablet and phone?
  **a** Spanish   **b** French   **c** Italian
3 What device can't she live without?
  **a** tablet   **b** camera   **c** phone
4 How many photos do people take every year?
  **a** one million   **b** one billion   **c** one trillion
5 How many televisions do people in the U.S. have?
  **a** 116 million   **b** 123 million   **c** 26 million

**5** ▶ **5.10**  Watch or listen to the rest of the show. Complete the sentences with the words in the box.

headphones   DVR   car   laptop   tablet   music

Simon

Parminder

Vincent

1  Simon can't live without _____ or his _____ .

2  Parminder can't live without her _____ and _____ .

3  Vincent can't live without his _____ and his _____ .

**6** ▶ **5.10**  Watch or listen again. Choose the correct options to complete the sentences.

1  Parminder uses her devices for *presentations / letters / games*.
2  She uses her devices *on the weekend / at night / every day*.
3  Vincent can play *the piano / the violin / the guitar*.
4  His car is from *1962 / 1967 / 1972*.
5  Simon travels *by underground / on foot / by car*.

**7** ▶ **5.11**  Listen to Vincent's sentence. Is it easy to hear the underlined words? Why?

> And when I get home, I watch TV at night.

🧩 **Listening builder** | sentence stress

In English, we stress the important words in sentences. You can usually understand the general idea if you only hear these words.
*I play basketball on Fridays with a women's team.*
*I work for a big company, and we use all the top technology.*

**8  A** ▶ **5.12**  Read the Listening builder. Read and listen to sentences 1–4. Can you understand them?

1  _____ can't live without _____ phone. _____ _____ call people _____ take photos.
2  _____ brother's _____ doctor. _____ usually goes _____ _____ hospital _____ car.
3  Kevin wants _____ new laptop, _____ _____ very expensive.
4  _____ _____ morning, _____ always listen _____ _____ radio.

**B** ▶ **5.12**  Listen again and complete the sentences with the unstressed words.

**9**  In pairs, talk about your electronic devices. Answer the questions.

1  What do you use your devices for?
2  Which device can't you live without? Why not?
A  *I use my phone to listen to music and take photos. What about you?*
B  *I don't use my phone to take photos. I have a good camera.*

## 5C  I love it!

**1** Match the words in the box with pictures a–f.

bike riding   walking   cleaning   swimming   reading   cooking

**Go to Vocabulary practice:** activities, page 119

**2 A** Write two activities in each column.

| 😊 I love … | 😄 I like … | 😕 I don't like … | 😣 I hate … |
|---|---|---|---|
| | | | |

**B** Tell your partner about what you love, like, don't like, and hate.

**A** *I love cooking.*      **B** *Really? I hate cooking. I love going out!*

**3 A** Look at the pictures on the webpage. What activities can you see?

**B** Read the text. Complete the sentences with *loves*, *likes*, *doesn't like*, and *hates*.

1  Midori _____ listening to music. She _____ Taylor Swift.
2  Laura _____ grocery shopping.
3  Diego _____ visiting his grandpa.
4  Josh _____ sleeping late because he _____ early mornings.
5  Ellie _____ watching movies with her friends, and she _____ popcorn.

---

That's ⓘnteresting    **LIKES AND DISLIKES**

*I like listening to music. Taylor Swift is my favorite singer. I love her!*
♥ 4      **Midori**

*I like watching movies with my friends. We always have a big bowl of popcorn – I love it!*
♥ 6      **Ellie**

*My brother and I don't like grocery shopping. Mom always takes us on the weekend!*
♥ 7      **Laura**

*I love visiting my grandpa. I can always talk to him, and he helps me a lot.*
♥ 12      **Diego**

*I love sleeping late on weekends. Early mornings? I hate them!*
♥ 3      **Josh**

**4 A** Match the object pronouns in **bold** with the people and things. Read the text again and check.

1  I love **her**!
2  Mom always takes **us** on the weekend!
3  I can always talk to **him**.
4  He helps **me** a lot.
5  I hate **them**!
6  I love **it**!

a  Diego
b  early mornings
c  Taylor Swift
d  popcorn
e  Laura and her brother
f  Diego's grandpa

**B** Choose the correct words to complete the sentences. Then read the Grammar box.

1  We use object pronouns instead of *people and things / times and places*.
2  We use object pronouns *before / after* verbs.

---

📖 **Grammar**    **object pronouns**

| Subject pronouns: | Object pronouns: | |
| --- | --- | --- |
| I | me | *I don't understand. Can you help **me**?* |
| you | you | *Are **you** Adam? This is for **you**.* |
| he | him | ***He** isn't friendly. I don't like **him**.* |
| she | her | ***She** works in your office. Do you know **her**?* |
| it | it | ***It's** perfect. I love **it**!* |
| we | us | ***We're** in the yard. Can you see **us**?* |
| they | them | ***They're** new here. I don't know **them**.* |

---

Go to Grammar practice: object pronouns, page 100

**5 A** ▶ 5.15  **Pronunciation:** the /h/ sound Listen and repeat. Pay attention to the /h/ sound.

him    her    he    help    happy

**B** ▶ 5.16  Say the questions and sentences. Then listen, check, and repeat.

1  Do you like him?    **2**  I can't see her.    **3**  He hates horses.    **4**  Hi, Harry. How are you?

**6** ▶ 5.17  Complete the conversation with object pronouns. Listen and check.

A  Do you like Emma Stone?
B  Yes, I do. I love ¹_____ . She's great!
A  What about Bruno Mars?
B  Yes, I like ²_____ too.
A  Do you like shopping for clothes?

B  No, I hate ³_____ .
A  Do you like Monday mornings?
B  No, I hate ⁴_____ .
A  What do you think of cats?
B  I don't like ⁵_____ , but they like ⁶_____ !

Go to Communication practice: Student A page 138, Student B page 146

**7 A** Write three examples in each of the circles.

singers and bands    actors    food and drink    animals    activities

**B** In pairs, ask and answer questions about the people and things.

Do you like …?    What about …?    What do you think of …?

**8** Tell the class about you and your partner.

*We both love cats. I like Ryan Gosling, but Carla doesn't like him.*

**Personal Best**   Write a conversation like the one in exercise 6 between you and someone in your family.

## 5D My profile

**1 A** Look at the profile on the "CityMeet" app. What do you think you can do with the app?

a find an apartment in a city    b make new friends in a city    c find a new job in a city

**B** Read the profile and check.

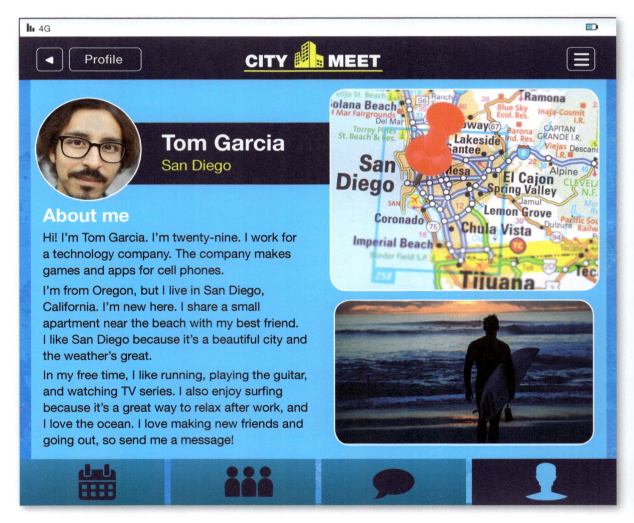

**2** Read the profile again. Complete the sentences with the correct words.

1 Tom works for a _____ company.
2 He's from _____ , but he lives in _____ .
3 He lives near the _____ with his _____ .
4 He thinks the weather in San Diego is _____ .

5 He plays the _____ and watches _____ in his free time.
6 He loves making _____ .

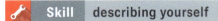

### Skill    describing yourself

**When you write a text to describe yourself, use a different paragraph for each topic.**

- personal information about you and your job: *Hi! My name's Marta. I'm a teacher.*
- where you live: *I live in Rio. I share an apartment with my best friend.*
- what you do in your free time: *In my free time, I like listening to music and cooking for friends.*
- information about your family: *I have a brother. His name's Paulo, and he's 18.*

**3** Read the Skill box. Check (✔) the topics that are in Tom's profile.

a his job ☐    b where he lives ☐    c his family ☐    d his free-time activities ☐

**4** Complete Kimberley's profile with sentences a–c.

   **a** I also love traveling because it's a great way to meet new people.

   **b** I study French and Spanish. I can also speak Portuguese.

   **c** We love San Diego because it's a fun and exciting city.

# ABOUT ME

Hello! I'm Kimberley Watson, and I'm a student at the University of San Diego. ¹____

I live in a house with four friends. We're all students. ²____

In my free time, I like watching French movies, running, and going out with my friends. ³____

**5** Imagine Tom and Kimberley meet on CityMeet. Do they become friends? Choose an option and complete the sentence.

Tom and Kimberley *become / don't become* friends because _____ .

### ✦ Text builder | *because*

**We use *because* to give a reason. It answers the question *Why?***

*I like San Diego **because** it's a beautiful city.*

*Why do you like traveling?*   ***Because** it's a great way to meet new people.*

**6 A** Read the Text builder and find sentences with *because* in Tom and Kimberley's profiles. How do you say *because* in your language?

   **B** Match 1–5 with a–e. Make sentences with *because*.

| | | | |
|---|---|---|---|
| **1** | I live in a small apartment | **a** | I'm usually tired after work. |
| **2** | I go to work by bus | **b** | it's good exercise. |
| **3** | I like swimming | **c** | it's quiet and the people are friendly. |
| **4** | I don't often go to the gym | **d** | houses in the city are expensive. |
| **5** | I like living in a small town | **e** | I can't drive. |

**7** Complete the sentences with your own ideas.

   **1** I love my city/town because _____ .

   **2** I'm often tired in the evening because _____ .

   **3** I like cooking because _____ .

   **4** I don't often go out because _____ .

   **5** I usually get up early because _____ .

**8 A** **PREPARE** Plan an online profile for you. Decide what information to include. Make notes about:

- your personal information
- your work or study
- where you live and who you live with
- your free-time activities and why you like them

   **B** **PRACTICE** Write your profile. Use one paragraph for each topic. Remember to use *because* to give reasons.

   **C** **PERSONAL BEST** Read your partner's profile. Does each paragraph contain one topic? Choose a paragraph that you like and tell your partner why you like it.

# Hello   The verb *be* (*I*, *you*)

We use the verb *be* to give information about people.

*I'm Carlos and I'm a teacher.*

We usually use contractions in affirmative and negative forms.

*You're a student.* = You are a student.   *I'm not in Class 3.* = I am not in Class 3.

We form negatives with *not* or the contraction *n't*.

| ▶ 1.4 | I | you |
|---|---|---|
| + | I**'m** a student. | You**'re** a teacher. |
| – | I**'m not** a teacher. | You**'re not** a student. |
| ? | **Am** I in Class 2? | **Are** you in my class? |
| Y/N | Yes, I **am**. / No, I**'m not**. | Yes, you **are**. / No, you**'re not**. |

## 1A   The verb *be* (*he*, *she*, *it*)

We use *he*, *she*, and *it* to talk about a person or a thing.

*The teacher is Mexican. He's from Puebla.*   *My car's not from Germany. It's from Japan.*

We usually use contractions in affirmative and negative forms. We form negatives with *not* or the contraction *n't*.

*Akemi's not / Akemi isn't Chinese.* = Akemi is not Chinese.
*She's Japanese.* = She is Japanese.

| ▶ 1.14 | he | she | it |
|---|---|---|---|
| + | Leo**'s** from Peru. | Lucía**'s** Colombian. | The book**'s** Chinese. |
| – | He**'s not** / He **isn't** from Chile. | She**'s not** / She **isn't** Argentinian. | It**'s not** / It **isn't** Italian. |
| ? | **Is** Ravi from India? | **Is** Ayla Turkish? | **Is** the car German? |
| Y/N | Yes, he **is**. / No, he**'s not** / he **isn't**. | Yes, she **is**. / No, she**'s not** /she **isn't**. | Yes, it **is**. / No, it**'s not** / it **isn't**. |

## 1C   The verb *be* (*we*, *you*, *they*)

We use *we*, *you*, and *they* to talk about people and things in the plural.

*The engineers are here. They're from India.*   *Susan and I are not happy. We're sad.*

We usually use contractions in affirmative and negative forms. We form negatives with *not* or the contraction *n't*.

*You're in Class 3.* = You are in Class 3.
*The pizzas aren't expensive.* = The pizzas are not expensive.

| ▶ 1.29 | we | you | they |
|---|---|---|---|
| + | We**'re** 25 years old. | You**'re** doctors. | They**'re** French. |
| – | We**'re not** old. | You**'re not** chefs. | Ana and Bea **are not** / **aren't** here. |
| ? | **Are** we sad? | **Are** you happy? | **Are** they in Class 4? |
| Y/N | Yes, we **are**. / No, we**'re not**. | Yes, you **are**. / No, you**'re not**. | Yes, they **are**. / No, they**'re not**. |

**1**   Choose the correct words to complete the sentences and questions.

1 I *'m* / *'re* Harry.
2 You *'m* / *'re* Lola.
3 *Am* / *Are* you a student?
4 *Am I* / *I'm* in Room 3.
5 *Are you* / *You are* late?
6 No, I *'m not* / *aren't*.
7 *Am* / *Are* I in this class?
8 Yes, you *am* / *are*.

◀ Go back to page 4

**1**   Complete the sentences with the correct words.

1 This is my friend Daniel. He _____ from Spain.
2 Anna's not in class today. _____'s at home.
3 Sophie _____ a student. She's the teacher.
4 This is my car. _____'s a Toyota.
5 A Where _____ Ryan Gosling from?
  B He _____ from Canada.
6 A What's the capital of Australia? Is _____ Sydney?
  B No, it _____ . It's Canberra.
7 A _____ María from Colombia?
  B No, she _____ . She's from Mexico.
8 A Is sushi from Japan?
  B Yes, _____ is.

◀ Go back to page 7

**1**   Rewrite the sentences. Change the words in **bold** to *we*, *you* or *they*.

1 **Elsa and Lucy** are police officers.
_____
2 **Maite and I** are 21 years old.
_____
3 Are **you and Wei** from China?
_____
4 **The doctors** are not from India.
_____
5 Where are **Maggie and Jake Gyllenhaal** from?
_____
6 How old are **you and your friend**?
_____

**2**   Choose the correct words to complete the questions and sentences.

1 We *'s not* / *'re not* doctors.
2 *Is* / *Are* Ismail from Turkey?
3 Sam and I *am* / *are* in London.
4 I *'m not* / *'re not* your teacher.
5 Where *is* / *are* the actor from?
6 Ana and Rosa *is* / *are* from Spain.

◀ Go back to page 11

## 2A Singular and plural nouns

We use *a* and *an* with singular nouns. We use *a* with nouns that start with consonants (*b, d, f, g*, etc.) and we use *an* with nouns that start with vowels (*a, e, i, o, u*).

*It's a book.    She's an actor.*

To make a noun plural, we usually add *-s* or *-es*.

*a key ⇨ three keys    a watch ⇨ two watches*

| ▶ 2.3 | Singular | Plural |
| --- | --- | --- |
| | It's **an** umbrella. | They're umbrella**s**. |
| | I'm **a** waitress. | We're waitress**es**. |

**Spelling rules for plurals**

We usually add *-s* to nouns to make a plural.

*bag ⇨ bags*

When a noun ends in a consonant + *y*, we remove the *y* and then add *-ies*.

*country ⇨ countries*

When a noun ends in **ch**, **sh**, **s**, or **x**, we add *-es*.

*watch ⇨ watches*

Some plurals are irregular.

*child ⇨ children    man ⇨ men    woman ⇨ women    person ⇨ people*

## 2A *this, that, these, those*

We use *this* and *these* + the verb *be* to identify things that are near us.

*This is my purse and these are my sunglasses.*

We use *that* and *those* + the verb *be* to identify things that are not near us.

*That's my school and those are my friends.*

| ▶ 2.4 | Things that are near | Things that are not near |
| --- | --- | --- |
| Singular | **This** is my wallet. | **That**'s my teacher. |
| Plural | **These** are my books. | **Those** are my classmates. |

**Look!** We can also use *this/that/these/those* + noun. *That book is new.*

## 2C Possessive adjectives, *'s* for possession

We use possessive adjectives before nouns to say that something belongs to someone.

*Joseph is my brother.    This is our house.*

We use the same possessive adjectives for singular and plural nouns.

*Is that your key?    Are those your keys?*

| ▶ 2.11 | Possessive adjectives |
| --- | --- |
| my | I'm French. **My** wife is Spanish. |
| your | Are **you** sad? **Your** boyfriend's not here. |
| his | **He**'s a teacher. **His** students are young. |
| her | **She**'s an actor. **Her** house is big. |
| its | **It**'s a small restaurant. **Its** pizzas are good. |
| our | **We**'re late. **Our** boss isn't happy. |
| their | **They**'re tour guides. **Their** jobs are interesting. |

If we talk about possession with a name or a noun, we add *'s* to the name or noun.

*Is that the teacher's book?    Are you Rob's sister?*

---

**1** Complete the sentences with singular or plural nouns and *a* or *an*, if necessary.

| Singular | Plural |
| --- | --- |
| **1** It's a city. | They're _____ . |
| **2** She's _____ . | They're actors. |
| **3** Are you a waitress? | Are you _____ ? |
| **4** He's not _____ . | They're not children. |
| **5** It's a watch. | They're _____ . |
| **6** It's not _____ . | They're not umbrellas. |
| **7** I'm a woman. | We're _____ . |
| **8** He's _____ . | They're people. |

**2** Match the parts to make sentences and questions.

1 Alice is an _____        a tour guide.
2 It's an _____           b IT worker.
3 He's a _____            c umbrella.
4 Jo and I are _____      d engineers.
5 Are you a _____         e sunglasses?
6 Where are my _____      f chef?

◀ Go back to page 14

**1** Choose the correct words to complete the sentences.

1 *This / These* is my room.
2 Excuse me. Are *that / those* your glasses?
3 Look! Is *this / that* your phone over there?
4 Are *these / this* your keys?
5 Is *that / those* your pen, or is it my pen?
6 Are *these / this* your credit cards?

◀ Go back to page 15

**1** Complete the sentences with the correct possessive adjectives.

1 Hello. _____ name's Kate.
2 We're from Lima. This is a photo of _____ house.
3 He's French. _____ name is Olivier.
4 They're British, but _____ parents are from Peru.
5 Hi, I'm Tom. What's _____ name?
6 This is Luisa and _____ husband, Sven.

**2** Complete the sentences with *'s* for possession so they mean the same as the first sentences.

1 She's Olivia. Those are her sunglasses.
   Those are *Olivia's sunglasses*  .
2 He's my son. That's his credit card.
   That's _____ .
3 This is my daughter. Her name is Ruby.
   My _____ .
4 She's our doctor. Her phone number is 665342.
   Our _____ .

◀ Go back to page 19

## 3A Simple present (*I, you, we, they*)

We use the simple present to talk about facts and routines.

*I drink coffee for breakfast.*
*We eat a lot of fruit.*

We form negatives with *don't* (*do not*) + the base form of the verb (*eat, have, play,* ...).

*My parents don't like tea.*
*They don't eat meat.*

We form questions with *do* + subject + the base form of the verb.

*Do you like fish?*
*Do they have breakfast?*

| ▶ 3.3 | I / you / we / they |
|---|---|
| + | I **have** a big breakfast.<br>You **eat** a lot of fruit. |
| – | We **don't drink** coffee.<br>They **don't like** cheese. |
| ? | **Do** you **have** a big breakfast?<br>**Do** they **eat** fish? |
| Y/N | Yes, I **do**. / No, I **don't**.<br>Yes, they **do**. / No, they **don't**. |

**1** Complete the sentences with the correct form of the verbs in parentheses.

1 I _____ pizza. (like)
2 We _____ eggs or cheese. (not eat)
3 They _____ lunch at home. (not have)
4 You _____ tea. (drink)
5 Our children _____ green vegetables. (not like)
6 My husband and I _____ a lot of fruit. (eat)
7 I _____ coffee at night. (not drink)
8 You _____ breakfast. (not have)

**2** Order the words to make questions. Then complete the short answers.

1 you / meat / eat / do
_____ ? No, I _____ .
2 you / do / food / like / Indian
_____ ? Yes, we _____ .
3 potatoes / they / like / do
_____ ? Yes, they _____ .
4 drink / do / you and Anna / coffee
_____ ? No, we _____ .

◀ Go back to page 25

## 3C Simple present (*he, she, it*)

For *he, she* and *it*, we often add *-s* to the base form to make the affirmative form.

*I drink tea for breakfast.* ⇨ *He drinks tea for breakfast.*

| Spelling rules for simple present verbs with *he, she, it* |
|---|
| We usually add *-s* to the base form.<br>*work ⇨ works* |
| When a verb ends in a consonant + *y*, we remove the *y* and then add *-ies*.<br>*study ⇨ studies* |
| When a verb ends in *ch*, *sh*, *s*, or *x*, we add *-es*.<br>*watch ⇨ watches* |
| Some verbs are irregular.<br>*go ⇨ goes    do ⇨ does    have ⇨ has* |

We form negatives with *doesn't* (*does not*) + the base form of the verb.

*My sister doesn't speak English.*

We form questions with *does* + subject + the base form of the verb.

*Does our teacher work on weekends?*

| ▶ 3.14 | he / she / it |
|---|---|
| + | Kevin **exercises** in the morning.<br>She **lives** in Boston. |
| – | He **doesn't want** a new car.<br>My house **doesn't have** a yard. |
| ? | **Does** he **live** in Chicago?<br>**Does** Sandra **go** to the gym? |
| Y/N | Yes, he **does**. / No, he **doesn't**.<br>Yes, she **does**. / No, she **doesn't**. |

**1** Write the simple present *he, she, it* form of the verbs.

1 like _____
2 have _____
3 play _____
4 eat _____
5 go _____
6 try _____
7 drink _____
8 wash _____

**2** Rewrite the sentences. Use affirmative (+), negative (–) or question (?) forms.

1 My father makes good cakes.
_____ (?)
2 Anna doesn't go to college.
_____ (+)
3 Mark works on Tuesdays.
_____ (–)
4 Does she have two children?
_____ (+)
5 Sam thinks about soccer all day.
_____ (?)
6 My sister doesn't watch TV in the evening.
_____ (+)

◀ Go back to page 29

# 4A Frequency adverbs

We use frequency adverbs with the simple present to talk about routines.

*They always go to the gym on Friday.*
*I sometimes play soccer on the weekend.*

Frequency adverbs come before most verbs, but we put frequency adverbs after the verb *be*.

*I usually have lunch at work.*
*I'm always at home in the evening.* **NOT** ~~I always am at home in the evening.~~

| ▶ 4.3 | Frequency adverbs | |
|---|---|---|
| always | He **always** takes a shower in the morning. | 100% |
| usually | Julia **usually** gets up early. | |
| often | You **often** get home after 9:00 p.m. | |
| sometimes | I'm **sometimes** late for class. | |
| never | My parents **never** drink coffee. | 0% |

**Look!** *never* has a negative meaning, but we use a affirmative form.
*My children never get up early.* **NOT** ~~My children don't never get up early.~~

# 4C Simple present: *wh-* questions

We ask questions with question words to ask for specific information.

A day / time of day – *When does your brother go to the gym?*
A time – *What time does the class start?*
A thing – *What do you drink at work?*
A person – *Who do you work with?*
A place – *Where do you live?*
A reason – *Why do you get up early on Saturday?*
A number – *How many keys do you have?*
An age – *How old is Julian?*
A manner – *How do you get to work?*

The word order in questions with most verbs is question word + *do/does* + subject + main verb + rest of question.

| ▶ 4.8 | Question word | *do/does* | Subject | Main verb | Rest of question |
|---|---|---|---|---|---|
| | What | do | you | have | for breakfast? |
| | When | does | she | see | her friends? |
| | Where | do | his parents | work? | |

With the verb *be*, the word order in questions is question word + *am/is/are* + subject + rest of question.

| ▶ 4.9 | Question word | *am/is/are* | Subject | Rest of question |
|---|---|---|---|---|
| | Why | am | I | cold? |
| | What time | is | the bus? | |
| | How | are | you | today? |

**1** Order the words to make sentences.

1 brother / never / my / up / gets / early

_____ .

2 office / I / have / usually / lunch / at / the

_____ .

3 trains / late / always / the / night / at / are

_____ .

4 always / the / morning / a / take / I / in / shower

_____ .

5 dressed / I / get / usually / breakfast / before

_____ .

6 friendly / very / is / teacher / my / always

_____ .

7 never / we / dinner / before / have / 9:00 p.m.

_____ .

8 videos / watch / sometimes / in / we / class

_____ .

◀ Go back to page 33

**1** Complete the questions with the question words in the box.

> How many    What    What time
> When    Where    Why

1 _____ does your brother do?
   He's a taxi driver.
2 _____ do you usually play tennis?
   I usually play on the weekend.
3 _____ does your sister work?
   She works at the hospital.
4 _____ do you like your job?
   Because I meet a lot of people and it's interesting.
5 _____ does your English class start?
   At 7:30 p.m.
6 _____ cousins do you have?
   I have eight cousins.

**2** Write questions.

1 What / you / want for dinner?

_____

2 Why / she / ride her bike to work?

_____

3 Who / be / your favorite actors?

_____

4 How / they / know that man?

_____

5 Where / your brother / go grocery shopping?

_____

6 What time / the lesson / finish?

_____

◀ Go back to page 37

## 5A  *can* and *can't*

We use *can* and *can't* (*cannot*) to talk about ability.

*I can play the piano.     My grandmother can't drive.*

To make questions with *can*, we put *can* before the subject.

*Can you speak Portuguese?     What can he cook?*

We use the same form for all people and things.

*I/You/He/She/It/We/They can swim.*

| ▶ 5.3 | I / you / he / she / it / we / they |
|---|---|
| + | I **can speak** Italian. |
| – | You **can't play** the violin. |
| ? | **Can** he **cook** Chinese food? |
| Y/N | Yes, he **can**. / No, he **can't**. |

**Look!** We use *can/can't* with *well* to say we are good/bad at something.
*She can speak English well.*
*They can't swim well.*

**1** Write affirmative (+) or negative (–) sentences with *can*.

1 My sister / drive. (–)

_____

2 Dogs / swim. (+)

_____

3 Her son / use a computer. (–)

_____

4 My dad / cook well. (+)

_____

**2** Complete the questions. Use *can* and the verbs in brackets. Then write the short answers.

1 A _____ Sarah _____ five kilometers? (run)
  B Yes, _____ .
2 A _____ you and Jo _____ salsa? (dance)
  B No, _____ .
3 A _____ your son _____ Italian food? (cook)
  B Yes, _____ .
4 A _____ you _____ well? (sing)
  B No, _____ .

◀ Go back to page 43

## 5C  Object pronouns

The object of a sentence is the noun which comes after the verb.

*I like cookies.* (*cookies* are the object of the sentence)
*Ana calls her sister every week.* (*her sister* is the object of the sentence)

We use object pronouns instead of nouns when we know what the noun is.

*Emily is a really nice person. I like her.* (*her* = Emily)
*Fruit juice is good for you. I drink it for breakfast.* (*it* = fruit juice)

| ▶ 5.14 | Subject pronouns | Object pronouns | |
|---|---|---|---|
| | I | me | I'm here. Can you see **me**? |
| | you | you | You're friendly. I like **you**. |
| | he | him | Paul's a doctor. We work with **him**. |
| | she | her | Who is Karen? I don't know **her**. |
| | it | it | I love hiking. Do you like **it**? |
| | we | us | We're at work. Call **us** if you have a problem. |
| | you | you | You and Ben are only 12 years old. Your parents take care of **you**. |
| | they | them | I have three cats. I love **them**! |

**Look!** We always use object pronouns, not subject pronouns, after prepositions.
*Can you come with me?*
*Where's Paul? I want to talk to him.*

**1** Replace the underlined words with object pronouns.

1 I love <u>books</u>.                    _____
2 My sister has <u>the car</u>.           _____
3 He doesn't like <u>Maria</u>.           _____
4 They cook for <u>my wife and me</u>.    _____
5 Give the book to <u>John</u>.           _____
6 Can he help <u>you and Abdul</u>?       _____

**2** Choose the correct words to complete the sentences.

1 Ivan's a waiter. I see *he / him* at work.
2 Lucy lives in France, but *she / her* isn't French.
3 I hate cleaning. Why do I do *me / it*?
4 Your children are quiet. Where are *they / them*?
5 This bike is very fast. Do you want *it / them*?
6 Can you take care of my plant? *It / Her* needs water every day.

◀ Go back to page 47

# Hello Classroom language

1 ▶ 1.7 Listen and repeat.

**1** Open your books.

**2** Close your books.

**3** Turn to page 5.

**4** Look at the picture.

**5** Listen and repeat.

**6** Work in pairs.

**7** Excuse me, what does "nice" mean?

**8** I'm sorry, I don't understand.

**9** How do you say "bom dia" in English?

**10** Can you repeat that, please?

**11** How do you spell that?

**12** Sorry I'm late.

2 Complete the conversation with the words in the box.

> turn   open   listen   ~~late~~   look   spell   work   close   mean   repeat

**Norio** Hello. Sorry I'm ¹___late___ .
**Teacher** Hello. Are you Norio?
**Norio** Yes, I am.
**Teacher** I'm your teacher. My name's Helen.
**Norio** Hi.
**Teacher** ²_____ your book and turn to page 6, please.
**Norio** I'm sorry, can you ³_____ that?
**Teacher** Yes. ⁴_____ to page 6 in your book.
**Norio** OK.

**Teacher** ⁵_____ at the picture of a family.
**Norio** Excuse me, what does "family" ⁶_____ ?
**Teacher** Your mother, father, brothers, sisters …
**Norio** I understand. How do you ⁷_____ "family"?
**Teacher** F-A-M-I-L-Y.
**Norio** Thank you.
**Teacher** ⁸_____ and repeat – "family".
**Norio** Family.
**Teacher** Very good. Now, ⁹_____ your books and ¹⁰_____ in pairs …

## 1A  Countries and nationalities

1  ▶ 1.12 Listen and repeat.

| | | | | | |
|---|---|---|---|---|---|
| 1  Argentina Argentinian | 2  Brazil Brazilian | 3  Canada Canadian | 4  Chile Chilean | 5  China Chinese | 6  Colombia Colombian |

| | | | | | |
|---|---|---|---|---|---|
| 7  France French | 8  Germany German | 9  India Indian | 10  Italy Italian | 11  Japan Japanese | 12  Mexico Mexican |

| | | | | | |
|---|---|---|---|---|---|
| 13  Peru Peruvian | 14  Russia Russian | 15  Spain Spanish | 16  Turkey Turkish | 17  the UK British | 18  the U.S. American |

2  Look at the pictures. Complete the sentences with the correct country or nationality.

1  Lionel Messi is _____ .

2  Paris is in _____ .

3  A kimono comes from _____ .

4  Pasta is _____ food.

5  A panda is an animal from _____ .

6  Washington, D.C., is the capital of _____ .

7  Machu Picchu is in _____ .

8  These are _____ dolls.

9  The Taj Mahal is in _____ .

10  Rio de Janeiro is a _____ city.

◀ Go back to page 6

## 1B Jobs

1 ▶ 1.19 Listen and repeat.

1 an actor

2 a chef

3 a doctor

4 an engineer

5 an IT worker

6 an office worker

7 a police officer

8 a receptionist

9 a salesclerk

10 a singer

11 a student

12 a taxi driver

13 a teacher

14 a tour guide

15 a TV host

16 a waiter/a waitress

> **Look!** We use *an* with jobs that begin with vowels (*a, e, i, o, u*) and *a* with jobs that begin with consonants (*b, c, d, f*, etc.).
> I'm **a** teacher.
> Are you **an** office worker?

2 Match the jobs in the box with objects 1–8. Use *a* or *an*.

waiter   salesclerk   engineer   singer   receptionist   doctor   chef   actor

1 _____

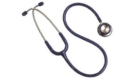

2 _____

3 _____

4 _____

5 _____

6 _____

7 _____

8 _____

◀ Go back to page 8

## 1C Adjectives (1)

1 ▶ 1.32 Listen and repeat.

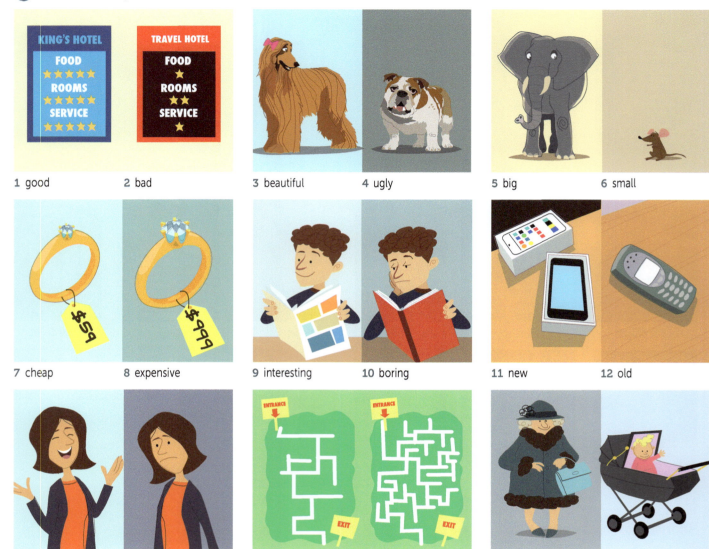

1 good        2 bad        3 beautiful        4 ugly        5 big        6 small

7 cheap        8 expensive        9 interesting        10 boring        11 new        12 old

13 happy        14 sad        15 easy        16 difficult        17 old        18 young

2 Choose the correct words to complete the conversations.

A This phone is ¹cheap / boring.
It's only $50.
B Yes, but it's not ²difficult / good.
Look at this phone.
A It's $795! It's very ³expensive / new.

A How ⁶good / old is Michael?
B He's ⁷new / young. He's three years
old today!
A He's very ⁸happy / sad.

A Hi, Sara. Do you understand Italian?
B Yes. I'm Spanish, but Italian is
⁴big / easy for me.
A Oh, that's ⁵interesting / ugly.

A Wow – this painting is
⁹beautiful / difficult!
B Yes, but it's very ¹⁰bad / small.
A My house is small, too!

## 2A Personal items

1 ▶ 2.2 Listen and repeat.

1 a backpack
2 a book
3 a camera
4 a cell phone
5 a change purse

6 a credit card
7 glasses
8 keys
9 a pen
10 a pencil

11 a purse
12 a tablet
13 an umbrella
14 a wallet
15 a watch

2 Write the items you can see in the pictures.

1 _____
2 _____
3 _____

4 _____
5 _____
6 _____

◀ Go back to page 14

## 2B Colors

1 ▶ 2.8 Listen and repeat.

1 black
2 blue
3 brown
4 gold
5 gray

6 green
7 orange
8 pink
9 purple

10 red
11 silver
12 white
13 yellow

2 Write the colors.

1 red + blue = _____
2 red + white = _____
3 blue + yellow = _____

4 black + white = _____
5 red + yellow = _____
6 red + blue + yellow = _____

◀ Go back to page 16

## 1C Numbers 0–100

1 ▶ 1.26 Listen and repeat.

| | | | | | |
|---|---|---|---|---|---|
| 0 zero | 5 five | 10 ten | 15 fifteen | 20 twenty | 50 fifty | 100 a hundred/ |
| 1 one | 6 six | 11 eleven | 16 sixteen | 21 twenty-one | 60 sixty | one hundred |
| 2 two | 7 seven | 12 twelve | 17 seventeen | 22 twenty-two | 70 seventy | |
| 3 three | 8 eight | 13 thirteen | 18 eighteen | 30 thirty | 80 eighty | |
| 4 four | 9 nine | 14 fourteen | 19 nineteen | 40 forty | 90 ninety | |

2 Write the numbers as words or digits.

1 34 _____   3 63 _____   5 88 _____   7 29 _____   9 12 _____
2 _____ seventy-two   4 _____ ninety-one   6 _____ fifty-seven   8 _____ forty-four   10 _____ a hundred

◀ Go back to page 10

## 2C Family and friends

1 ▶ 2.10 Listen and repeat.

1 grandfather    2 grandmother

3 grandparents

4 mother    5 father    7 son    8 daughter

6 parents    9 children

10 husband    11 wife    12 sister    13 brother    14 boyfriend    15 girlfriend

2 Look at the family tree. Read the sentences and write the names.

1 My brother is Liam. _____
2 Julia is my wife. _____
3 My sister is Julia, and my brother is George. _____
4 My girlfriend is Molly. _____
5 My parents are George and Gloria, and my sister is Molly. _____
6 Bob is my father, and Mark and George are my brothers. _____
7 My wife is Judith. _____
8 My husband's brother is Mark. _____
9 Our children are Julia, Mark, and George. _____ and _____
10 Our parents are Judith and Bob. _____ , _____ and _____

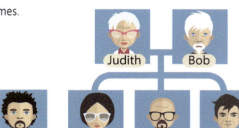

Judith    Bob

Tony    Julia    Mark    George    Gloria

Ben    Molly    Liam    Lucy

◀ Go back to page 18

## 3A Food and drink

1 ▶ 3.2 Listen and repeat.

**Food**

1 bread
2 cake
3 cheese
4 chicken
5 potato chips

6 chocolate
7 cookies
8 eggs
9 fish
10 French fries

11 fruit
12 ice cream
13 meat
14 pasta
15 pizza

16 potatoes
17 rice
18 salad
19 sandwich
20 vegetables

**Drinks**

21 coffee
22 milk
23 orange juice
24 tea
25 water

**Look!** If we want to talk about the food and drink that we eat and drink at breakfast, lunch, and dinner, we can use the verb *have*.
*What do you* **have** *for breakfast/lunch/dinner?*
*I* **have** *coffee for breakfast. I* **have** *a sandwich for lunch. I* **have** *fish for dinner.*

8:00 a.m.    1:00 p.m.    6:30 p.m.

have breakfast        have lunch        have dinner

2 Choose the correct words to complete the sentences.

1 Ice cream has *milk / cheese* in it.
2 Potatoes are *fruit / vegetables*.
3 Cake, cookies, and *chocolate / salad* are bad for you.
4 Chips and French fries come from *potatoes / pasta*.
5 British people have *rice / milk* in their tea.

6 Spaghetti is a type of *bread / pasta*.
7 I have *breakfast / lunch* at 8:00 a.m.
8 Vegetarians don't eat *meat / salad*.
9 I drink *orange juice / fish* in the morning.
10 I have *chocolate / meat* and vegetables for dinner.

◀ Go back to page 24

## 3C Common verbs (1)

1 ▶ 3.12 Listen and repeat.

1 **exchange** money

2 **exercise**

3 **go** to school

4 **have** two children

5 **know** the answer

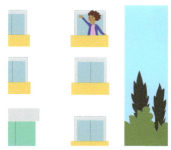

6 **live** in an apartment

7 **make** coffee

8 **say** "goodbye"

9 **study** German

10 **think** (about …)

11 **use** a tablet

12 **want** a drink

13 **watch** a movie

14 **work** in an office

> **Look!** We use *make* for food and drink:
> *I make a sandwich every day.*
> *We make dinner for our friends.*
>
> We use *think* for thoughts and opinions:
> *I think about work. (thought)*
> *We think it's a good idea. (opinion)*

2 Choose the correct words to complete the sentences.

1 After work, I *know / go / use* to the gym.
2 I *study / say / live* English and Spanish in college.
3 I *make / do / work* dinner for my family every evening.
4 I *think / know / work* in a restaurant – I'm a waitress!
5 A Do you like that book?
   B No, I *think / watch / use* it's boring.
6 My boyfriend and I *watch / say / live* TV in the evening.

7 Do you *exchange / exercise / study* at the gym?
8 Do they *use / know / live* in a big house?
9 I *study / live / say* "good morning" to people at work.
10 My cell phone is old. I *watch / want / work* a new one.
11 A What's the capital of China?
   B I don't *go / use / know*.
12 My children *use / say / make* the Internet a lot.

◀ Go back to page 28

## 4A Daily routine verbs

1 ▶ 4.2 Listen and repeat.

1 get up

2 take a shower

3 get dressed

4 leave home

5 start work

6 go grocery shopping

7 listen to the radio

8 do housework / do homework

9 finish work

10 get home

11 go to bed

12 read a book

2 Complete the text with the correct form of the verbs in the box.

do (x2)   get (x3)   go (x2)   leave   finish   listen   start   take

I'm Miranda, and this is my typical day. I <sup>1</sup>_____ up at 7:00 in the morning and <sup>2</sup>_____ a shower. Then I have breakfast with my son, Leon. He <sup>3</sup>_____ dressed, and then we <sup>4</sup>_____ home at about 8:30 a.m. Leon goes to school, and I'm an office worker. I <sup>5</sup>_____ work at 9:00 a.m.
I <sup>6</sup>_____ work at 3:00 p.m. and go to Leon's school. We <sup>7</sup>_____ grocery shopping and <sup>8</sup>_____ home at about 4:00 in the afternoon. In the evening, Leon <sup>9</sup>_____ his homework and I make dinner. After dinner, Leon <sup>10</sup>_____ to bed at 8:00 p.m. and I <sup>11</sup>_____ housework and <sup>12</sup>_____ to the radio. I go to bed at 11:00 p.m. … and the next day, we do it all again!

◀ Go back to page 32

## 4B Transportation

1 ▶ 4.6 Listen and repeat.

**1** by bike

**2** by boat

**3** by bus

**4** by car

**5** by ferry

**6** by motorcycle

**7** by plane

**8** by taxi

**9** by train

**10** by truck

**11** on foot

**12** on the subway/Underground/metro

> **Look!** Different cities have different names for their underground trains.
> *In New York, I go on the **subway**.    In London, I go on the **underground**.    In Sydney, I go on the **metro**.*

2 Match the types of transportation in the box with the pictures.

> truck   taxi   subway   ferry   train   plane   boat   motorcycle

| | | | |
|---|---|---|---|
| | | | |

3 Complete the sentences with the correct types of transportation and *by* or *on*.

1 I go _____  to the train station. Then I go _____ downtown. After that, I go _____ to the office.

2 Lucia goes _____ to the airport. Then she goes _____ to New York. After that, she goes downtown _____ .

3 We go _____ to Boston, but my brother goes _____ . Then we all go _____ to Provincetown.

◀ Go back to page 34

## 3B  Days and times of day

1  ▶ 3.7 Listen and repeat.

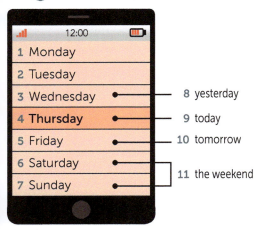

| 12:00 |
|---|
| **1** Monday |
| **2** Tuesday |
| **3** Wednesday |
| **4** Thursday |
| **5** Friday |
| **6** Saturday |
| **7** Sunday |

8 yesterday
9 today
10 tomorrow
11 the weekend

6:00 a.m. – 12:00 p.m.
**12** morning

12:00 p.m. – 6:00 p.m.
**13** afternoon

6:00 p.m. – 9:00 p.m.
**14** evening

9:00 p.m. – 5:00 a.m.
**15** night

**Look!** We use the preposition *on* with days of the week and *the weekend*, *in* with *the morning*, *the afternoon*, and *the evening*, and *at* with *night*.
*I eat fish* **on** *Friday.*
*I go grocery shopping* **on** *the weekend.*
*I have breakfast* **in** *the morning.*
*I drink milk* **at** *night.*

We also say *on* + day and time of day:
**on** *Wednesday morning,* **on** *Friday afternoon, etc.*

2  Chose the correct words to complete the sentences and questions.

1 My birthday's *on / in / at* Sunday.
2 I have dinner *on / in / at* the evening.
3 We don't drink coffee at *afternoon / evening / night*.
4 I have lunch with Emma on *the afternoon / Friday / the morning*.
5 Is your English class *on / in / at* Thursday evening?

6 They have breakfast at 9:00 in *the weekend / Wednesday / the morning*.
7 Is Marcus on vacation *on / in / at* Thursday?
8 They don't have classes *on / in / at* Wednesday afternoons.
9 What do you eat on the *afternoon / weekend / the night*?
10 On Sunday, I have chicken for lunch *on / in / at* the afternoon.

◀ Go back to page 26

## 4C  Adjectives (2)

1  ▶ 4.7 Listen and repeat.

1 cold   2 hot

3 clean   4 dirty

5 fast   6 slow

7 friendly   8 unfriendly

9 nice   10 horrible

11 large   12 small

13 long   14 short

15 noisy   16 quiet

2  Complete the text with the adjectives in the box.

noisy   cold   quiet   hot   short   friendly   dirty   large

Hi, I'm Matt. I'm a student in Seattle, Washington. I always get up at 8:30 and I have a ¹_____ tea for breakfast. Then, I go to school on foot. It's sometimes ²_____ in the mornings, but that's OK – it's only a ³_____ walk.

I live in a ⁴_____ house with eight students. They're really ⁵_____ . We always make dinner together, and sometimes there are a lot of ⁶_____ dishes when we finish! My roommates play music, and the house is sometimes ⁷_____ , so I usually work in the library – it's always ⁸_____ there.

◀ Go back to page 36

## 5A Common verbs (2)

1 ▶ **5.1** Listen and repeat.

1 **arrive** at the airport

2 **call** my mother

3 **take care of** my daughter

4 **cook** fish

5 **dance** salsa

6 **drive** a car

7 **give** a gift

8 **help** my grandmother

9 **meet** friends

10 **play** soccer

11 **play** the piano

12 **sing**

13 **speak** Italian

14 **swim** in the ocean

15 **travel** by bus

2 Complete the sentences with the correct form of the verbs in the box.

| cook   meet   give   arrive   help   drive   speak   play (x2)   travel   sing   call   take care of |

1 Simon _____ Portuguese.
2 I _____ dinner on the weekend.
3 Sharon often _____ basketball.
4 My father _____ a bus.
5 I always _____ my son with his homework.
6 We usually _____ by train.
7 I sometimes _____ my friend's dog.
8 We _____ in Lima at 9:15 a.m.
9 I always _____ Lucy for a coffee after work.
10 You never _____ me flowers.
11 Jo likes music. She _____ and _____ the guitar.
12 My parents live in India, so I _____ them on Skype.

◀ Go back to page 42

## 5B Electronic devices

**1** ▶ **5.8** Listen and repeat.

**1** desktop computer

**2** DVD player

**3** earphones

**4** GPS

**5** headphones

**6** laptop

**7** radio

**8** remote control

**9** smartphone

**10** smart speaker

**11** tablet

**12** TV (television)

**2** ~~Cross out~~ the word which is incorrect in each sentence.

**1 A** Listen to this song on my phone – it's great!
　**B** Hold on – I need some *earphones / remote control / headphones*.

**2 A** Can I check my e-mail?
　**B** Yes. You can use my *radio / tablet / smartphone*.

**3 A** My friend lives on Bridge Street, but I don't know where that is.
　**B** It's OK. I have a *smartphone / GPS / headphones*. We can use that.

**4 A** Do you want to watch a movie tonight?
　**B** We can't. I don't have a *remote control / TV / DVD player*.

**5 A** I work at home. I have a *laptop / TV / desktop computer* and that's all I need.
　**B** At home? What a nice job!

**6 A** It's quiet. Why don't we listen to some music?
　**B** OK ... here's my *radio / GPS / smart speaker*.

**7 A** The news is on at 12:00.
　**B** OK, the *DVD player / TV / radio* is over there.

**8 A** Do you have a TV?
　**B** No, I don't. I watch TV shows on my *laptop / radio / smartphone*.

◀ Go back to page 44

## 5C Activities

1 ▶ 5.13 Listen and repeat.

1 bike riding

2 cleaning

3 cooking

4 dancing

5 going out

6 hiking

7 listening to music

8 meeting friends

9 reading

10 running

11 shopping

12 sleeping

13 swimming

14 watching TV/movies

> **Look!** We can use activities that end in -ing or nouns with the verbs *like*, *love*, and *hate*.
> *I like shopping.   I love clothes!*
> *I don't like bike riding.   I hate bikes.*

2 Match the activities in the box with pictures 1–8.

swimming   reading   running   cooking   bike riding   cleaning   shopping   sleeping

1 _____

2 _____

3 _____

4 _____

5 _____

6 _____

7 _____

8 _____

◀ Go back to page 46

# Hello  Student A

**1** Look at the labels. Ask Student B for the name of the city.

**A** *What's LHR?*
**B** *I think it's London.*
**A** *How do you spell that?*
**B** *L-O-N-D-O-N.*

FINAL DEST.
**LHR**
1 _____

FINAL DEST.
**MEX**
2 _____

FINAL DEST.
**IST**
3 _____

FINAL DEST.
**LAX**
4 _____

FINAL DEST.
**HGK**
5 _____

**2** Listen to Student B's airport codes. Tell him/her the correct city for the letters.

New Delhi   Cape Town   Barcelona   New York   Amsterdam

## 1A  Student A

**1** You are Mehmet. Answer Student B's questions with the information.

**B** *What's your name?*
**A** *I'm Mehmet Guliyev.*
**B** *How do you spell that?*
**A** *M-E-H-M-E-T ...*

| Name: | Mehmet Guliyev |
|---|---|
| Nationality: | Turkish |
| Phone: | 90 312 213 2965 |

**2** Ask Student B the questions and write down his/her answers.

1  What's your name?
_____

2  Where are you from?
_____

3  What's your phone number?
_____

## 1C  Student A

**1** Ask Student B questions about the Antarctic Zebras to complete the information.

*Where are they from?   How old is Bev?   What is her job?*

**The Antarctic Zebras**

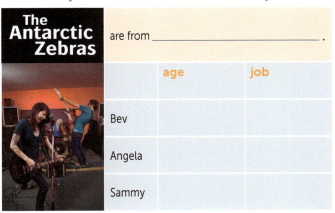

are from _____.

| | age | job |
|---|---|---|
| Bev | | |
| Angela | | |
| Sammy | | |

**2** Now look at the information about the Rocking Stones. Answer Student B's questions.

**The Rocking Stones**

are from Portland, in the U.S.

| | age | job |
|---|---|---|
| Kevin | 44 | police officer |
| Rob | 40 | engineer |
| Nick | 41 | chef |

## 2A  Students A and B

1  Look at the picture. In pairs, ask about the objects.
   *What's this/that?   What are these/those?*

2  Now, turn to page 143 and check your ideas.

## 2C  Student A

Ask and answer questions with Student B to complete David and Victoria Beckham's family tree.

A *What's David's mother's name?*
B *Her name is ...*

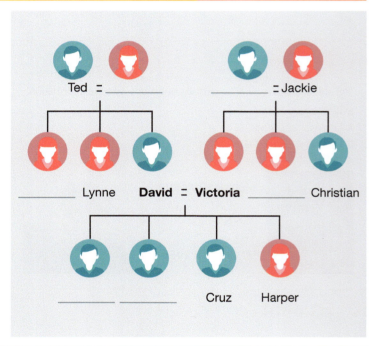

## 2D  Student A

1  Ask Student B the questions and write down the answers. Remember to be polite.

A *Excuse me, what time's the next train to Boston, please?*
B *It's at eleven forty-five.*
A *Thanks.*
1  What time's the next train to Boston?  _____
2  What's Lucy's phone number?  _____
3  Where's the teacher from?  _____
4  How old are you?  _____
5  What's the name of the café?  _____

2  Answer Student B's questions with the answers in the box.

> He's 28.    She's from Mexico.    You're in Room 48.
> It's F-O-S-T-E-R.    It's at 6:40.

## 3A  Student A

**1**  Ask Student B questions to complete the information.

A *What do you have for breakfast?*
B *For breakfast, I eat …*

| breakfast | lunch | dinner |
|-----------|-------|--------|
|           |       |        |

**2**  Look at the information. Answer Student B's questions about your breakfast, lunch, and dinner.

| breakfast | lunch | dinner |
|-----------|-------|--------|

## 3C  Student A

**1**  Ask Student B questions about Maggie to complete the information in the chart.

A *Does Maggie live in a city?*
B *Yes, she does. She lives in Sacramento.*

|                                      | Maggie | Antonio |
|--------------------------------------|--------|---------|
| work in an office?                   |        | ✗ (he / work / in a school) |
| live in a city?                      |        | ✓ |
| have children?                       |        | ✓ (he / have / two daughters) |
| watch TV in the morning?             |        | ✗ (he / work) |
| use public transportation every day? |        | ✓ |
| go to the gym after work?            |        | ✗ (he / make / dinner) |
| study in the evening?                |        | ✗ (he / watch / TV) |
| play sports on the weekend?          |        | ✓ |

**2**  Look at the information about Antonio. Answer Student B's questions and give extra information when you can.

B *Does Antonio work in an office?*     A *No, he doesn't. He works at a school.*

## 4A  Student A

**1**  Write sentences in the simple present with the frequency adverbs in parentheses. Then read them to Student B.

1  Leila / watch / movies on her phone. (sometimes)

_____

2  Dean / wake up / before 6:00 a.m. (often)

_____

3  Paulo / read / in bed. (usually)

_____

4  Marta / be / late for work. (never)

_____

5  Shaun / cook / dinner for his family. (always)

_____

**2**  Listen to Student B. Match the names in the box with the people.

Danny   Nina   Eric   Claire   Tom

| 1 _____ | 2 _____ | 3 _____ | 4 _____ | 5 _____ |
|---|---|---|---|---|
|  |  |  |  |  |
| *I usually finish work after 7:00 p.m.* | *I'm often at the library at night.* | *I always drink tea for breakfast.* | *I never take a bath in the morning.* | *I sometimes go to the gym on Saturdays.* |

136

## 4C Student A

**1** Ask Student B questions about Ella. Write his/her answers.

**A** *Where does Ella live?*     **B** *She lives in Philadelphia.*

**Ella**

**Questions**

| |
|---|
| Where / live? |
| What / do? |
| Where / work? |
| What time / get up? |
| What time / finish work? |
| Why / like her job? |
| How / relax in the evening? |
| What / do on the weekend? |

**2** Read Zain's profile. Listen to Student B and answer his/her questions.

**Zain**

Hi, I'm Zain. I live in Los Angeles. I'm a waiter at a big hotel in Hollywood. I get up at 8:00 a.m., and before work I usually go to the gym. I start work at 11:00, and I finish at 9:00 p.m. I like my job because I meet interesting people. To relax in the evening, I play the guitar. I usually work on the weekend.

## 4D Student A

**1** You are a customer. Ask Student B for the things on your shopping list. Then ask how much each thing is. Remember to be polite.

**A** *Good morning. Can I have a cheese sandwich, please?*
**B** *Here you are.*
**A** *Thank you. How much is it?*
**B** *$1.99. Anything else?*

Shopping list
1 cheese sandwich
6 eggs
some orange juice
some coffee
some pasta
Total price = ?

**2** You are a salesclerk. Serve Student B. Remember to be polite.

```
2x bottles water    $1.60
fish                $5.80
1x pizza (4 cheese) $3.99
1 box salad         $1.50
1 chocolate cake    $3.85
Total               $16.74
```

## 5A Student A

**1** Look at the chart. Ask questions with *can* to guess which person Student B has.

**A** *Can she drive?*
**B** *Yes, she can.*

| | Annie | Mona | Sara | Lucy | Hana | Kim |
|---|---|---|---|---|---|---|
| Can / drive? | ✗ | ✓ | ✓ | ✓ | ✓ | ✓ |
| Can / speak Spanish? | ✗ | ✓ | ✓ | ✗ | ✓ | ✗ |
| Can / play the guitar? | ✓ | ✗ | ✓ | ✗ | ✓ | ✗ |
| Can / cook Chinese food? | ✓ | ✓ | ✗ | ✓ | ✗ | ✗ |
| Can / dance salsa? | ✗ | ✗ | ✓ | ✗ | ✗ | ✓ |

**2** Answer Student B's questions about Mark. You can only say *Yes, he can* or *No, he can't.*

**MARK**

He can swim well and write computer programs.
He can't take care of children, play the piano, or speak French.

# 5C  Student A

**1**  Look at the profiles for a website called *New Friends*. Ask and answer questions with Student B to complete the information.

**A** *What does Daniela think about cooking?*     **B** *She likes it.*

☺☺ = love, ☺ = like, ☹ = not like, ☹☹ = hate

| Daniela | |
| --- | --- |
| | cooking |
| | cats and dogs |
| | early mornings |

| Bill | |
| --- | --- |
| | hiking |
| | housework |
| | books |

| Monica | |
| --- | --- |
| | going out |
| | bike riding |
| | movies |

| Miguel | |
| --- | --- |
| ☹ | cleaning |
| ☺☺ | reading |
| ☹☹ | sports |

| Claudio | |
| --- | --- |
| ☺ | swimming |
| ☺☺ | watching movies |
| ☹ | dancing |

| Lucy | |
| --- | --- |
| ☺ | sleeping |
| ☺ | animals |
| ☺☺ | food and drink |

**2**  Look at the profiles again. Find the best new friend for each person.

# Hello   Student B

**1** Listen to Student A's airport codes. Tell him/her the correct city for the letters.

> Hong Kong   Los Angeles   Mexico City   London   Istanbul

A *What's LHR?*
B *I think it's London.*
A *How do you spell that?*
B *L-O-N-D-O-N.*

**2** Look at the labels. Ask Student A for the name of the city.

FINAL DEST. **JFK**
1 _____

FINAL DEST. **BCN**
2 _____

FINAL DEST. **CPT**
3 _____

FINAL DEST. **DEL**
4 _____

FINAL DEST. **AMS**
5 _____

---

# 1A   Student B

**1** Ask Student A the questions and write down his/her answers.

1 What's your name?

_____

2 Where are you from?

_____

3 What's your phone number?

_____

**2** You are Saori. Answer Student A's questions with the information.

A *What's your name?*
B *I'm Saori Arakawa.*
A *How do you spell that?*
B *S-A-O-R-I ...*

| Name: | Saori Arakawa |
| --- | --- |
| Nationality: | Japanese |
| Phone: | 81 90 1790 1357 |

---

# 1C   Student B

**1** Look at the information about the Antarctic Zebras. Answer Student A's questions.

**The Antarctic Zebras** are from Chicago, in the U.S.

| | age | job |
| --- | --- | --- |
| Bev | 19 | student |
| Angela | 24 | IT worker |
| Sammy | 25 | tour guide |

**2** Now ask Student A questions about the Rocking Stones to complete the information.

*Where are they from?   How old is Kevin?   What is his job?*

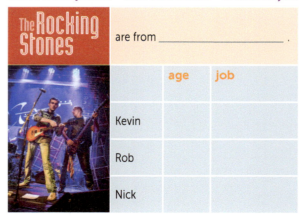

**The Rocking Stones** are from _____ .

| | age | job |
| --- | --- | --- |
| Kevin | | |
| Rob | | |
| Nick | | |

## 2A  Students A and B

Look at the picture. In pairs, discuss if you were right or wrong.

**A** *This is a pen.*
**B** *You're right.*

## 2C  Student B

Ask and answer questions with Student A to complete David and Victoria Beckham's family tree.

**B** *What's Victoria's mother's name?*
**A** *Her name is ....*

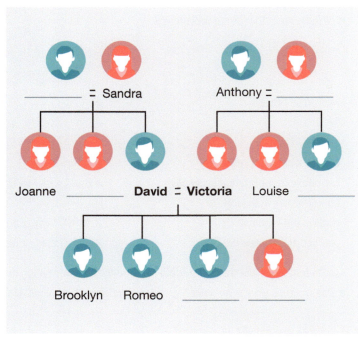

## 2D  Student B

**1**  Answer Student A's questions with the answers in the box.

> I'm 39.    It's 07700 900638.    The Oak Tree Café.
> It's at 11:45.    He's from Canada.

**2**  Ask Student A the questions and write down the answers. Remember to be polite.

**B** *Excuse me, what time's the flight to Los Angeles, please?*
**A** *It's at six forty.*
**B** *Thanks.*

**1**  What time's the flight to Los Angeles?    _____
**2**  How old is the teacher?    _____
**3**  Where's María from?    _____
**4**  What room am I in?    _____
**5**  How do you spell your last name?    _____

## 3A  Student B

**1** Look at the information. Answer Student A's questions about your breakfast, lunch, and dinner.

| breakfast | lunch | dinner |
|-----------|-------|--------|

**2** Ask Student A questions to complete the information.

B *What do you have for breakfast?*
A *For breakfast, I eat …*

| breakfast | lunch | dinner |
|-----------|-------|--------|
|           |       |        |

## 3C  Student B

**1** Look at the information about Maggie. Answer Student A's questions and give extra information when you can.

A *Does Maggie live in a city?*
B *Yes, she does. She lives in Sacramento.*

|  | Maggie | Antonio |
|---|---|---|
| work in an office? | ✓ | |
| live in a city? | ✓ (she / live / in Sacramento) | |
| have children? | ✗ (she / have / two cats) | |
| watch TV in the morning? | ✗ | |
| use public transportation every day? | ✗ (she / walk / to work) | |
| go to the gym after work? | ✓ | |
| study in the evening? | ✓ (she / study / English) | |
| play sports on weekends? | ✗ (she / make / cakes) | |

**2** Ask Student A questions about Antonio to complete the information in the chart.

B *Does Antonio work in an office?*     A *No, he doesn't. He works at a school.*

## 4A  Student B

**1** Listen to Student A. Match the names in the box with the people.

| Marta   Shaun   Leila   Dean   Paulo |

1 _____   2 _____   3 _____   4 _____   5 _____

*I often wake up before 6:00 a.m.*  *I'm never late for work.*  *I usually read in bed.*  *I sometimes watch movies on my phone.*  *I always cook dinner for my family.*

**2** Write sentences in the simple present with the frequency adverbs in parentheses. Then read them to Student A.

1 Claire / drink / tea for breakfast. (always)

_____

2 Tom / go / to the gym on Saturdays. (sometimes)

_____

3 Eric / take / a bath in the morning. (never)

_____

4 Danny / be / at the library at night. (often)

_____

5 Nina / finish / work after 7:00 p.m. (usually)

_____

# 4C  Student B

**1** Read Ella's profile. Listen to Student A and answer his/her questions.

A *Where does Ella live?*      B *She lives in Philadelphia.*

**Ella**

Hi, I'm Ella. I live in Philadelphia. I'm a teacher at a school downtown. I usually get up at 6:00 a.m. I start work at 8:30, and I finish at 5:00 p.m. I love my job because I like children. To relax in the evening, I watch TV with my family. On the weekend, I play a lot of sports.

**2** Ask Student A questions about Zain. Write his/her answers.

**Zain**

| Questions |
|---|
| Where / live? |
| What / do? |
| Where / work? |
| What time / get up? |
| What time / finish work? |
| Why / like his job? |
| How / relax in the evening? |
| What / do on the weekend? |

# 4D  Student B

**1** You are a salesclerk. Serve Student A. Remember to be polite.

A *Good morning. Can I have a cheese sandwich, please?*
B *Here you are.*
A *Thank you. How much is it?*
B *$1.99. Anything else?*

| | |
|---|---|
| 1 sandwich (cheese) | $1.99 |
| 6 eggs | $2.50 |
| orange juice | $1.80 |
| coffee | $3.29 |
| pasta | $1.50 |
| Total | $11.08 |

**2** You are a customer. Ask Student A for the things on your shopping list. Then ask how much each thing is. Remember to be polite.

Shopping list
2 bottles of water
some fish
1 four-cheese pizza
1 box of salad
1 chocolate cake
Total price = ?

# 5A  Student B

**1** Answer Student A's questions about Hana. You can only say *Yes, she can* or *No, she can't*.

A *Can she drive?*
B *Yes, she can.*

HANA

She can drive, speak Spanish, and play the guitar.
She can't cook Chinese food or dance salsa.

**2** Look at the chart. Ask questions with *can* to guess which person Student A has.

| | Sergio | Tom | Mark | Andy | Pete | Dennis |
|---|---|---|---|---|---|---|
| Can / take care of children? | ✓ | ✗ | ✗ | ✗ | ✓ | ✗ |
| Can / swim well? | ✗ | ✓ | ✓ | ✗ | ✓ | ✓ |
| Can / play the piano? | ✗ | ✗ | ✗ | ✗ | ✓ | ✗ |
| Can / speak French? | ✓ | ✓ | ✗ | ✓ | ✗ | ✗ |
| Can / write computer programs? | ✗ | ✗ | ✓ | ✗ | ✓ | ✗ |

## 5C  Student B

1  Look at the profiles for a website called *New Friends*. Ask and answer questions with Student A to complete the information.

**B** *What does Miguel think about cleaning?*  **A** *He doesn't like it.*

☺☺ = love, ☺ = like, ☹ = not like, ☹☹ = hate

| Daniela | |
|---|---|
| ☺ | cooking |
| ☺☺ | cats and dogs |
| ☹ | early mornings |

| Bill | |
|---|---|
| ☹ | hiking |
| ☹☹ | housework |
| ☺ | books |

| Monica | |
|---|---|
| ☹ | going out |
| ☹ | bike riding |
| ☺ | movies |

| Miguel | |
|---|---|
| | cleaning |
| | reading |
| | sports |

| Claudio | |
|---|---|
| | swimming |
| | watching movies |
| | dancing |

| Lucy | |
|---|---|
| | sleeping |
| | animals |
| | food and drink |

2  Look at the profiles again. Find the best new friend for each person.

# Irregular verbs

| Infinitive | Simple past |
|---|---|
| be | was, were |
| become | became |
| begin | began |
| break | broke |
| bring | brought |
| buy | bought |
| choose | chose |
| come | came |
| cost | cost |
| do | did |
| drink | drank |
| drive | drove |
| eat | ate |
| fall | fell |
| feel | felt |
| find | found |
| fly | flew |
| get | got |
| give | gave |
| go | went |
| have | had |
| hear | heard |
| hold | held |
| hurt | hurt |
| keep | kept |
| know | knew |

| Infinitive | Simple past |
|---|---|
| leave | left |
| lose | lost |
| make | made |
| meet | met |
| pay | paid |
| put | put |
| read (/riːd/) | read (/red/) |
| ride | rode |
| run | ran |
| say | said |
| see | saw |
| sell | sold |
| sit | sat |
| sleep | slept |
| spend | spent |
| speak | spoke |
| stand | stood |
| swim | swam |
| take | took |
| teach | taught |
| tell | told |
| think | thought |
| understand | understood |
| wake | woke |
| wear | wore |
| win | won |
| write | wrote |

# Personal
# Best

**Workbook**

## A1
Beginner

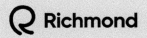
Richmond

# My life

**HELLO** ─ **LANGUAGE**

## GRAMMAR: The verb *be* (*I, you*)

**1** Match 1–7 with a–g.

| | | | |
|---|---|---|---|
| 1 | _____ you a student? | a | Yes |
| 2 | Yes, I _____. | b | not |
| 3 | No, I'm _____. | c | I'm a |
| 4 | _____, you are. | d | Are |
| 5 | No, you _____. | e | 're not |
| 6 | _____ student. | f | You're |
| 7 | _____ a teacher. | g | am |

**2** ▶1.1 Complete the sentences. Listen and check.

A Good morning. ¹_____ you a student?

B Oh, hello. Yes, I ²_____.

A Welcome to the school. My name's John. I'm a teacher here. And you ³_____ ... ?

B ⁴_____ Veronica. Nice to meet you. ⁵_____ I in your class?

A No, you ⁶_____. I'm ⁷_____ your teacher. ⁸_____ in Min's class.

B OK, thank you.

## VOCABULARY: Classroom language

**3** Match sentences 1–6 with pictures a–f.

1 Excuse me, what does this word mean? ____*f*____

2 I'm sorry, I don't understand. _____

3 How do you say "*arigatou*" in English? _____

4 Can you repeat that, please? _____

5 How do you spell that? _____

6 Sorry I'm late. _____

**4** Order the words to make sentences.

1 8 / to / books / page / open / your

_____

2 books / close / your

_____

3 turn / 7 / page / to

_____

4 at / look / picture / the

_____

5 and / listen / repeat

_____

6 in / pairs / work

_____

## PRONUNCIATION: The alphabet

**5** ▶1.2 Write the other letters of the alphabet. Listen and check.

| | | | |
|---|---|---|---|
| 1 | /eɪ/ | n**a**me | Aa, Hh, ____, ____ |
| 2 | /iː/ | s**ee** | Bb, Cc, ____, ____, ____, ____, ____, ____ |
| 3 | /ɛ/ | b**e**d | Ff, ____, ____, ____, ____, ____ |
| 4 | /ay/ | **I**'m | ____, ____ |
| 5 | /ow/ | n**o** | |
| 6 | /uː/ | y**ou** | Qq, ____, ____ |
| 7 | /ɑ/ | **a**re | |

## GRAMMAR: The verb *be* (*he*, *she*, *it*)

**1** Choose the correct words to complete the sentences.

1 A *Are / Is* that Donnie Yen?
B Yes, *it / you* is.

2 A Where *am / is* he from?
B *He's / It's* from Hong Kong.

3 A *Am / Is* this restaurant good?
B Yes! *He's / It's* great!

4 A She *'s not / 're not* from Britain. Where's she from?
B *He's / She's* from Chile.

5 A Where *is / are* you from?
B *I'm / It's* from Valletta.

6 A *Where's / Where are* Paris?
B *It's / She's* in France.

7 A *Is / Are* that the Turkish flag?
B No, it *is / 's not*.

8 A Spain's flag *am / is* red and yellow.
B Yes, *I'm / you're* right.

**2** (▶)1.3 Complete the sentences. Listen and check.

1 I _____ from Peru.

2 Where _____ she from?

3 He _____ American; he's Canadian.

4 _____ you Elena?

5 This _____ Junko. She _____ from Japan.

6 I _____ not Argentinian.

7 You _____ from Argentina. _____ you from Chile?

8 I think he _____ from India.

## VOCABULARY: Countries and nationalities

**3** Complete the chart.

| Country | Nationality |
|---|---|
| 1 _____ | Canadian |
| Chile | 2 _____ |
| China | 3 _____ |
| France | 4 _____ |
| 5 _____ | German |
| 6 _____ | Indian |
| Italy | 7 _____ |
| Peru | 8 _____ |
| Russia | 9 _____ |
| 10 _____ | British |
| the U.S. | 11 _____ |
| Turkey | 12 _____ |

**4** Complete the sentences with the correct country or nationality.

1 It's the flag of T _urke_ y. (country)

2 It's the I_ndia_ n flag. (nationality)

3 It's the S_____h flag.

4 It's the flag of C_____a.

5 It's the M_____n flag.

6 It's the C_____n flag.

7 It's the flag of B_____l.

8 It's the flag of the _____.

## PRONUNCIATION: Word stress

**5** (▶)1.4 Is the stress on the nationality and country the same (S) or different (D)? Listen, check, and repeat.

1 Argentina    Argentinian    _S_
2 China        Chinese        _D_
3 Germany      German         _____
4 Italy        Italian        _____
5 Mexico       Mexican        _____
6 Turkey       Turkish        _____
7 Brazil       Brazilian      _____
8 Japan        Japanese       _____

## LISTENING: Listening for information about people

**1** ▶ 1.5 Listen and complete the sentences with the words in the box.

> addresses   countries   ~~first names~~
> jobs   nationalities   numbers   last names

1 They are _first names_ .
2 They are _____ .
3 They are _____ .
4 They are _____ .
5 They are _____ .
6 They are _____ .
7 They are _____ .

**2** ▶ 1.6 Listen to two conversations. Where are the people?

**3** ▶ 1.6 Listen again. Complete the forms.

|  | Student 1 | Student 2 |
|---|---|---|
| **First name** | 1 _____ | Yasin |
| **Last name** | Aleksandrov | 5 _____ |
| **Nationality** | 2 _____ | Turkish |
| **Job** | 3 _____ | 6 _____ |
| **Classroom** | 4 _____ | 7 _____ |
| **Teacher** | Sandrine | 8 _____ |

**4** ▶ 1.7 Listen and correct any contractions.

1 A What is his job?          _What's_
  B He is a student.          _He's_

2 A You are not from Argentina, are you?          _____
  B I am from Argentina!          _____

3 A It is not in classroom 8. It is in classroom 10.          _____
  B Where is that?          _____

4 A What is her nationality?          _____
  B She is from Canada.          _____

5 A You are a good singer!          _____
  B No, I am not.          _____
  A You are!

6 A I am in Shenzhen.          _____
  B Where is Shenzhen?          _____
  A It is in China.          _____

**5** Look at the pictures and complete the job titles.

1 a__ __ __ __
2 e__ __ __ __ __ __ __
3 s__ __ __ __ __ __
4 l__ w__ __ __ __ __
5 r__ __ __ __ __ __ __ __
6 s__ __ __ __ __ __ __
7 s__ __ __ __ __
8 t__ __ __ __ g__ __ __ __
9 T__ h__ __ __ __
10 w__ __ __ __ __ __

## GRAMMAR: The verb *be* (*we*, *you*, *they*)

**1** Match sentences 1–10 with missing verbs a–c.

1 _____ the books expensive?

2 You and Harpinder _____ good friends.

3 Ursula, Frank, and the other students _____ in room 24.

4 _____ we in this classroom today?

5 They _____ sad; they are happy.

6 Liu and I _____ students from China.

7 You _____ a teacher. You're a student.

8 _____ you from Mexico?

9 We _____ the same age. He's 18 and I'm 20.

10 All the chefs here _____ Turkish.

    **a** are

    **b** 're not

    **c** Are

**2** Look at the examples. Write sentences with pronouns.

1 her name = Marta
*It's Marta.*

2 Keith and Sally ≠ American
*They're not American.*

3 I ≠ a police officer
_____

4 Pedro and Gabriela = from Brazil?
_____

5 you and Aubert = happy?
_____

6 you and I ≠ old.
_____

7 Elena = 25
_____

8 Michael = in Italy?
_____

9 Yuki and Natsuki = from Japan
_____

10 the book = interesting?
_____

## VOCABULARY: Numbers 11–100 and adjectives (1)

**3** Write the words for the next two numbers in 1–6.

1 twelve, thirteen, fourteen,
_____, _____ (15, 16)

2 twenty-four, twenty-six, twenty-eight,
_____, _____ (30, 32)

3 one hundred, ninety, eighty,
_____, _____ (70, 60)

4 eleven, twenty-two, thirty-three,
_____, _____ (44, 55)

5 sixty-seven, seventy-three, seventy-nine,
_____, _____ (85, 91)

6 ninety-nine, eighty-five, seventy-one,
_____, _____ (57, 43)

**4** ▶ 1.8 Complete the conversations with the correct adjectives. Listen and check.

1 **A** Are the shoes big?
  **B** No, they're very _____.

2 **A** That house is ugly.
  **B** Yes, it's not _____.

3 **A** Is he a _____ singer?
  **B** Yes. He's not bad.

4 **A** You don't look happy.
  **B** No, I'm not. I'm _____.

5 **A** The TV host is really boring!
  **B** Yes, she's not very _____.

6 **A** Is that watch $89? That's expensive!
  **B** Yes, it's not _____.

7 **A** This exercise is _____.
  **B** No it's not. It's easy.

8 **A** You're very _____, aren't you, Grandpa?
  **B** No, I'm not! I'm young!

## PRONUNCIATION: Numbers

**5** ▶ 1.9 Listen and choose the correct numbers.

1 13      30

2 14      40

3 15      50

4 $16      $60

5 17      70

6 18      80

7 $19      $90

8 40      42

9 52 km    62 km

10 83      93

## WRITING: Filling out a form

**1** Look at the picture and read the e-mail. Then fill out the form for Noemí.

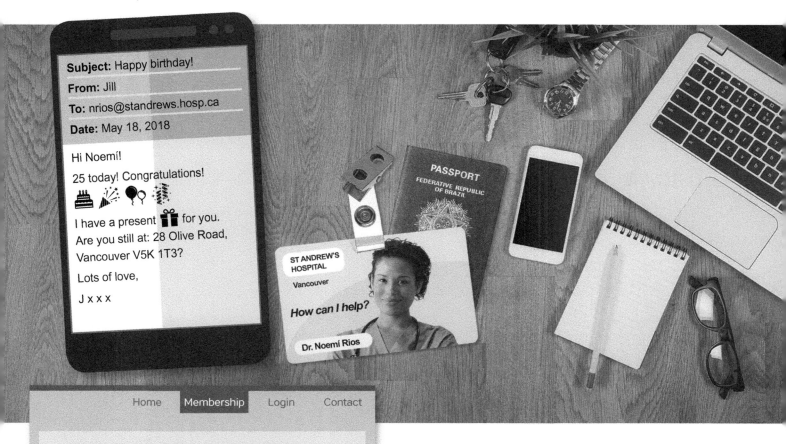

**Subject:** Happy birthday!

**From:** Jill

**To:** nrios@standrews.hosp.ca

**Date:** May 18, 2018

Hi Noemí!

25 today! Congratulations!

I have a present 🎁 for you.
Are you still at: 28 Olive Road,
Vancouver V5K 1T3?

Lots of love,

J x x x

ST ANDREW'S HOSPITAL
Vancouver
*How can I help?*
Dr. Noemí Rios

Home    Membership    Login    Contact

### To join the gym, fill out your personal information.

| | |
|---|---|
| Title | 1 *Dr.* |
| First name | 2 |
| Last name | 3 |
| Address line 1 | 4 |
| Address line 2 | |
| City | 5 |
| Zip code | 6 |
| E-mail address | 7 |
| Phone number | 8 *604-509-6995* |
| Nationality | 9 |
| Profession | 10 |
| Date of birth (MM/DD/YYYY) | 11 |

Send

**2** Read the form. Then correct the capitals in the sentences below.

| First name | Porfirio |
|---|---|
| Last name | Cubillos |
| Home city | Guadalajara |
| Nationality | Mexican |
| Country of residence | France |
| Married? | Yes |
| Wife's name | Claudine |
| Languages | Spanish, French, English |

1  my name is porfirio cubillos.

2  i'm from guadalajara in mexico, but i am in france now.

3  my wife, claudine, is french.

4  at home, we speak spanish and french.

**3** Write similar sentences for you. Remember to use capital letters correctly.

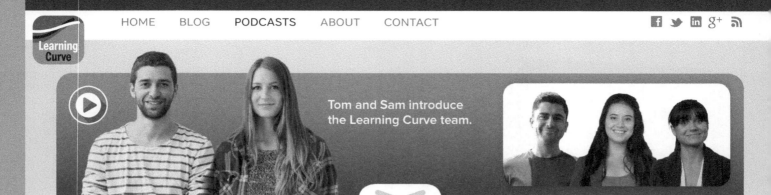

HOME  BLOG  PODCASTS  ABOUT  CONTACT

Tom and Sam introduce the Learning Curve team.

## LISTENING

**1** ▶ 1.10 Listen to the podcast about people at Learning Curve. In what order do the people speak? Write 1–5.

- a Jack _____
- b Penny _____
- c Tom ___1___
- d Taylor _____
- e Sam _____

**2** ▶ 1.10 Listen again. Match the people with the information.

| | | | |
|---|---|---|---|
| 1 | Tom | _____ | a is a chef. |
| 2 | Sam | _____ | b is from the U.S. |
| 3 | Taylor | _____ | c is a host of Learning Curve. |
| 4 | Penny | _____ | d works with Tom. |
| 5 | Jack | _____ | e is British and Argentinian. |

**3** ▶ 1.10 Listen again. Are the sentences true (T) or false (F)?

1 Every episode of Learning Curve is about food or travel. _____
2 Taylor also presents Learning Curve. _____
3 Taylor is from the U.S. _____
4 Penny lives in New York. _____
5 Sam has a restaurant. _____
6 Jack's last name is spelled G-O-O-D-E. _____

## READING

**1** Read Ethan's blog post about the city of Canberra. Match the people with photos a–c.

1 Chia _____
2 Bill _____
3 Karen _____

**2** Read the blog again. Check (✔) the correct sentences.

1 Canberra is the capital of Australia. _____
2 Canberra is an old city. _____
3 Chia's family are Chinese. _____
4 Chia is a doctor. _____
5 Bill's wife is from Canberra. _____
6 Houses in Canberra are cheap. _____
7 Karen thinks downtown is ugly. _____
8 It is easy to go from Canberra to the countryside. _____
9 Karen doesn't like the weather in Australia. _____

**3** Order the letters to make countries or nationalities. Write C or N.

1 A N C H I _____ _____
2 N A P H I S S _____ _____
3 Y U T E R K _____ _____
4 C A R N E F _____ _____
5 I N D A N A C A _____ _____
6 U R S A S I _____ _____
7 M A N G E R _____ _____
8 A N P A J _____ _____
9 C E M I X O _____ _____
10 G I A N T A R E N _____ _____

HOME  BLOG  PODCASTS  ABOUT  CONTACT

Our guest blogger this week is Ethan. He's in Australia!

# COOL CANBERRA!

**This week's guest blogger Ethan Moore goes to a fantastic city "down under"*...**

What is the capital city of Australia? Sydney? Melbourne perhaps? No, it's Canberra. Canberra's not big, like Sydney. And it's not as old as Melbourne. It's a new city, about a hundred years old. Its population is only 300,000 people. But it's a good city to live in. Three people who live here tell us why Canberra is so good.

Hi. My name's Chia. I love my city! My family is from China, but I'm Australian, too. Canberra is small, and the people are very friendly. It's great for shopping, and it's also very good for jobs. My friends all have good jobs here. They are doctors, receptionists, and IT workers. I'm an office worker – I work in a big building downtown. But it's only 15 minutes from my house.

Hello. I'm Bill and I'm 24. My wife and I are from Sydney. Sydney is a great city, but it's really expensive. A small house costs about $600,000! We can't afford that – I'm a teacher and my wife's a salesclerk. That's why we live in Canberra. It's not very cheap here, but it's less expensive than Sydney. Now we have a small house and we're very happy.

I'm Karen and I'm an engineer – hi! For me, Canberra is the perfect city because it's so beautiful. Downtown is very clean, and it's next to a big lake. You're never far from the countryside, and it's easy to get to – just ten minutes by car or on your bike! And of course the sky is blue, and the weather is perfect for being outside – it's Australia!

* If you go "down under", you go to Australia or New Zealand.

# People and things

## 2A LANGUAGE

**GRAMMAR: Singular and plural nouns; *this*, *that*, *these*, *those***

**1** Write the plural nouns.

1 She's a child.     They're _____.
2 It's a country.    They're _____.
3 It's a beach.      They're _____.
4 He's a person.     They're _____.
5 It's a nationality. They're _____.
6 She's a waitress.  They're _____.
7 She's a woman.     They're _____.
8 It's a box.        They're _____.

**2** (▶) 2.1 Look at the pictures. Complete the sentences with *this*, *that*, *these*, or *those*. Listen and check.

1 _____'s my doctor.

2 _____ is my backpack.

3 Are _____ your books?

4 Are _____ his pens?

5 Is _____ a dog?

6 _____ are beautiful dolls!

7 _____ is my house.

8 _____ are very old things.

**VOCABULARY: Personal objects**

**3** Order the letters to make personal objects.

1 His money is in his L A W T E L.                    _____
2 These S N A G L E S S U S are very expensive.       _____
3 You don't have any money? That's OK, you can pay by T R I C E D  D R A C. _____
4 I want to buy a small L E T B A T.                  _____
5 Do you have a M A R E C A to take pictures?         _____
6 She keeps her keys in her S U P E R.                _____

**4** Look at the pictures and complete the sentences.

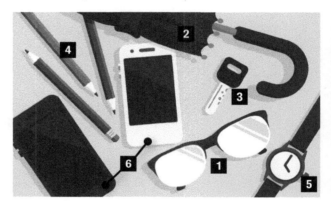

1 They're _____.
2 It's an _____.
3 It's a _____.
4 They're _____.
5 It's a _____.
6 They're _____.

**PRONUNCIATION: /ɪ/ and /iy/**

**5** (▶) 2.2 Which words in 1–10 have the sound /ɪ/? Listen and check.

1 a three      b six
2 a listen     b read
3 a this       b these
4 a picture    b police
5 a he         b it
6 a engineer   b teacher
7 a pen        b credit card
8 a cheap      b expensive
9 a easy       b difficult
10 a keys      b pencil

## READING: Preparing to read

**1** Complete the colors.

1 b __ __ __ k, b __ __ e, b __ __ __ n

2 g __ __ __ n, g __ __ y, g __ __ d

3 o __ __ __ __ e

4 p __ __ k, p __ __ __ __ e

5 r __ __

6 s __ __ __ __ r

7 w __ __ __ e

8 y __ __ __ w

**2** Look at the text and the photos. Then choose the correct answers.

1 Where is the text from?
   a a website          c a newspaper
   b a letter

2 What does *prized* mean in the title?
   a expensive          c special
   b old

3 Who wrote the text?
   a one person         b more than one person

**3** Read the text. Then read the sentences and write D (Danijela), M (Marko), C (Cheryl), or E (Eugenio).

1 This prized object is beautiful. _____

2 This person's object is big and goes everywhere with him or her. _____

3 These are expensive. _____

4 This object is from a grandparent. _____

5 His prized object is ugly. _____

6 His object helps him a lot. _____

7 Her prized object's old and new. _____

8 It's from his father and not small. _____

**4** Complete the sentences with the words in the box.

| very | ugly | prized | photos | old | object |
| it | is | isn't | glasses | family | expensive |
| earrings | difficult | beautiful | are | | |

1 Danijela says her _____ _____ _____.

2 Marko can't live without his _____.

3 Cheryl loves her album full of _____ _____.

4 Eugenio loves the painting, but _____ _____ _____.

5 And you? What is your _____ _____?

6 This exercise _____ _____ _____. It's easy!

### Our most prized objects

We all have objects we love for different reasons. Here are some people with their prized objects. And you? What's your special object?

#### Danijela, Slovenia

The important things in my life aren't objects; they're my friends and family. But I have a beautiful pair of earrings from my grandmother. They're not expensive, but I don't want to lose them.

#### Marko, Russia

I can't live without my glasses – they are my window to the world! Sometimes I can't find them, and it's difficult without them. They're a very expensive Italian pair. I've had these glasses for years, but they're still fantastic.

#### Cheryl, Philippines

My photo album is my most prized object. There are lots of family photos in it from when we were children. Some are twenty years old (they were my mother's), but I collected the photos in a new album last year. I take it with me everywhere.

#### Eugenio, Costa Rica

I love this painting of my great-grandfather (my grandfather's father). It's special because my father gave it to me. But my wife doesn't like it, and it's very big, so we don't have it in the house. It is a bit ugly, but I like it!

# GRAMMAR: Possessive adjectives; 's for possession

**1** Choose the correct words to complete the sentences.

1 Hi, *your / our / my* name's Nadya. Nice to meet you.

2 Rio de Janeiro is famous for *my / its / his* beaches.

3 That's Bozhi. He's a police officer. And that's *her / his / their* girlfriend with him.

4 We live in Sofia, but *our / your / its* home city is Varna.

5 And you? What's *my / her / your* name?

6 My parents live near the ocean. You can see it from *his / its / their* house.

7 What about you and your boyfriend? What are *your / his / my* jobs?

8 What's *our / your / her* job? Is she a doctor?

9 I'm a student. *Our / Their / My* classmates are great!

10 These are my dogs and that's *his / its / their* bed.

**2** Complete the sentences. Use *'s* for possession.

1 He's the teacher. Those are his books.
Those are *the teacher's* books.

2 This is my mother. That's her umbrella.
That's my _____ umbrella.

3 She's Anna. That's her room.
That's _____ room.

4 He's the tour guide. This is his camera.
This is the _____ camera.

5 That's Hugo. This is his laptop.
It's _____ laptop.

6 She's the engineer. Those are her keys.
Those are the _____ keys.

7 That's my friend. This is his wallet.
This is my _____ wallet.

8 He's the chef. That's his hat.
That's the _____ hat.

# VOCABULARY: Family and friends

**3** Read the text and choose the correct options to complete the sentences.

Hi! I'm Tuyen. This is my family. Hung is my [1] *daughter / husband / sister*, and we have two [2] *children / daughters / sons*. Their names are Nhung and Vien. Nhung is six and her little [3] *brother / sister / son* is three. Vien has the same name as his [4] *grandmother / grandfather / husband*, my father, but we live with my husband's [5] *grandchildren / parents / wives*. Hung's [6] *father's / son's / husband's* name is Tuan and Tuan's [7] *daughter / sister / wife* is named Thu. They're wonderful, and it's great for the children to live with their [8] *grandfathers / grandparents / girlfriends*.

Kim, my husband's [9] *mother / sister / wife*, also lives with us. She's the photographer! She's not married, but she has a [10] *boyfriend / wife / husband*. His name's Chi.

Tuan · Hung · Tuyen · Thu · Vien · Nhung

**4** Complete the sentences with the correct words.

1 Thu is Hung and Kim's _____.

2 Kim is Chi's _____.

3 Kim is Tuan and Thu's _____.

4 Thu is Nhung and Vien's _____.

5 Hung is Kim's _____.

6 Tuyen is Hung's _____.

7 Vien is Hung and Tuyen's _____.

8 Hung and Tuyen are Nhung and Vien's _____.

# PRONUNCIATION: 's

**5** ▶ 2.3 Say the sentences. Pay attention to the *'s* sound. Then listen, check, and repeat.

1 Is that George's mother?

2 They're Karina's sunglasses.

3 That watch is Haru's.

4 She's Pierre's sister.

5 Emma's cell phone is silver.

6 That's the doctor's son.

## SPEAKING: Telling the time

**1** (▶) **2.4** Listen to the three conversations. Then choose the correct options to complete the sentences.

1 The time now is
   a nine ten.
   b nine thirty.
   c nine twenty.

2 The movie starts at
   a eight oh-five.
   b seven forty-five.
   c eight o'clock.

3 The meeting usually finishes at
   a seven thirty.
   b nine thirty.
   c ten o'clock.

**2** (▶) **2.4** Listen again. What polite words do you hear? Check (✔) the words that you hear.

| | Conversation | | |
|---|---|---|---|
| | 1 | 2 | 3 |
| *Excuse me* | ✔ | | |
| *Please* | | | |
| *I'm sorry* | | | |
| *Thanks* | | | |
| *Thank you* | | | |

**3** In which conversation in exercise 1 and 2 is the person not polite?

**4** Read the answers and write the questions.

1 **A** What time/in Tokyo?

   _____

   **B** It's three a.m. there now.

2 **A** What time/train/to Boston?

   _____

   **B** It's in a half hour, at eleven ten.

3 **A** What time/your flight?

   _____

   **B** It's at six thirty.

4 **A** What time/now?

   _____

   **B** It's two forty-five.

5 **A** Excuse me, what/time?

   _____

   **B** I'm sorry, I don't know. I don't have a watch.

6 **A** What time/the class?

   _____

   **B** It's at five o'clock, in twenty minutes.

**5** Order the words to make sentences. Then match them with questions a–d.

1 forty-five / four / is / it / p.m. / there

   _____

2 about / in / minutes / one / ten / there's

   _____

3 almost / is / it / o'clock / twelve / here

   _____

4 a.m. / at / it / on / opens / Saturdays / ten

   _____

   a What time is the store open? _____
   b What's the time? _____
   c What time is it in Cairo? _____
   d What time's the next bus downtown? _____

HOME   BLOG   PODCASTS   ABOUT   CONTACT

Learning Curve

Tom and Sam talk about an online store.

## LISTENING

**1** ▶ 2.5 Listen to the podcast about an online store called "yourfavoritethings.com". Check (✔) the things you hear.

a watch     _____
b camera     _____
c tablet     _____
d sunglasses     _____
e pencils     _____
f keys     _____
g pen     _____
h umbrella     _____
i credit card     _____
j bag     _____

**2** ▶ 2.5 Listen again. Write T (true) or F (false).

1 Sam likes Tom's new watch.   _____
2 Tom's watch is cheap.   _____
3 Abbey's customers answer a lot of questions.   _____
4 Abbey gives Tom a small box.   _____
5 Tom lives in New York.   _____
6 Tom goes to the gym.   _____
7 Tom is never late.   _____
8 Abbey's customers only pay for the things they like.   _____
9 Tom likes Abbey's idea.   _____
10 The umbrella in the box costs $50.   _____

## READING

**1** Read Kate's blog about families. Choose the best summary for each person.

**Selma**

a Selma is unhappy because her parents are tired and poor.
b Selma is happy because she is going to college soon.
c Selma's family is not perfect, but she is happy.

**Nicolás**

a Nicolás is sad because his family has a small house and a small car.
b Nicolás likes being an only child because it's quiet and his family has money.
c Nicolás is happy because his parents are always out in the evenings.

**2** Choose the correct options to complete the sentences.

1 Kate's parents have *two / three / four* children.
2 Selma's parents spend a lot of money on *games / food / clothes*.
3 Selma goes out with her *brothers / parents / sisters*.
4 Selma is sad about leaving her *brothers and sisters / parents / friends*.
5 Nicolás thinks his parents have a(n) *easy / difficult / boring* life.
6 Nicolás's parents spend a lot of money on *taxis / presents / sports*.
7 Nicolás goes out with his *parents / grandparents / cousins*.

HOME    BLOG    PODCASTS    ABOUT    CONTACT

Our guest blogger this week is Kate.

# BIG family or small family?

Are you from a big family or a small family? My family's not big and it's not small. I only have one brother and no sisters. Some families have a lot of children, and other families only have one child. But which are better – big families with all the fun and noise, or small families with peace and quiet? Let's hear from two people with very different families, Selma and Nicolás.

**Selma:** I have two brothers and three sisters, and we all live with our parents. I'm eighteen years old, and the others are seventeen, fourteen, eleven, seven, and two. I think my mother and father are very tired! Having two sons and four daughters is expensive for our parents, and they never have any money. I think it's because my brothers eat so much! Our parents only own one expensive thing – a very big car! But I think big families are great for the children. My brothers and sisters are my friends, and we are like a team. We argue and fight sometimes, but at the end of the day, we are a family. My sisters and I go out together, and my younger brothers and sisters always play together. And with so many brothers and sisters, life is never boring! I start college in Germany next year, and I'm sad about leaving them.

**Nicolás:** I am an only child and it's great. I think my parents are happy, too! We live in a small house and our car's not big, but that means we have more money to spend on other things. Every year we fly to Argentina to see my grandmother, and my parents have money to enjoy their life. My father plays golf every weekend, and my mother goes to classes with her friends in the evening. Their lives aren't difficult! They buy me a lot of expensive presents, too! And I never need a taxi to get home from parties because my father drives me everywhere! Sometimes I wish I had brothers and sisters to talk to. But I'm not alone – I have my girlfriend, my cousins, and my friends to go out with. And everything is calm and quiet in my family. Big families are so noisy!

# Food and drink

**3A** LANGUAGE

## GRAMMAR: Simple present (*I*, *you*, *we*, *they*)

**1** Choose the correct words to complete the conversations.

1 **A** *Do you like / Are you like / You do like* this book?
   **B** Yes, I *do / eat / like*.

2 **A** *Are / Be / Do* your friends play tennis?
   **B** *Do they play / They do play / They play* tennis every Sunday.

3 **A** Fruit cake? No, thanks. I *don't want / want / do want* it.
   **B** Oh, really? *Do I love / I do love / I love* fruit cake!

4 **A** *Am / Do / Is* that food good?
   **B** No, it's not. Well, I *am not like / don't like / like* it.

5 **A** Where *do want you / do you want / you do want* to go?
   **B** Nowhere, thanks. I *don't have / have / do have* enough time.

6 **A** *Do you / Are you / You do* know Maria?
   **B** No, but *do I / I don't / I* know her sister, Bella.

**2** Rewrite the sentences. Use affirmative **(+)**, negative **(–)**, or question **(?)** forms.

1 I eat an apple every day.
   (–) *I don't eat an apple every day.*

2 We don't have class at eight o'clock.
   (+) _____

3 He is a taxi driver.
   (?) _____

4 Do they watch TV?
   (–) _____

5 They study English every day.
   (?) _____

6 Do you have a credit card?
   (+) _____

7 She is very happy.
   (–) _____

8 You speak Italian.
   (?) _____

## VOCABULARY: Food and drink

**3** Order the letters to make food and drink words.

1 Whole wheat D A B E R _____ W I N D C H A S E S _____ are good for you.

2 Does he drink O F F E C E _____ black or with L I K M _____?

3 Let's cook something quick like T A P S A _____.

4 I love the Z I P S A Z in Italy. _____.

5 Vegans don't eat T A M E _____ or S G E G _____.

6 Have some E T W A R _____ or A R N G O E  C E I J U _____.

**4** Look at the photos and complete the crossword.

## PRONUNCIATION: *do you* /dəyuw/

**5** ▶ 3.1 Listen and complete the questions. Repeat the questions.

1 _____ potato chips?

2 _____ cake?

3 _____ Turkish food?

4 _____ milk in China?

5 _____ dinner?

6 _____ for breakfast?

# LISTENING: Listening for times and days

**1** ▶ 3.2 Listen to the three conversations. Match the conversations with the places.

1 _____     **a** at a tourist information office
2 _____     **b** at a train station
3 _____     **c** at home
        **d** in a restaurant
        **e** in a store

**2** ▶ 3.2 Listen again. Check (✔) the days and times you hear.

| | Day | | | Time | | |
|---|---|---|---|---|---|---|
| **Conversation 1** | Thursday _____ | Friday _____ | | 7:15 _____ | 7:50 _____ | |
| **Conversation 2** | Tuesday _____ | Thursday _____ | | 9:00 _____ | 7:00 p.m. _____ | |
| **Conversation 3** | Monday _____ | Wednesday _____ | | 2:15 p.m. _____ | 2:50 p.m. _____ | |

**3** ▶ 3.3 Listen to six conversations and complete the sentences.

1 One orange juice _____ two teas, please.
2 What day's good _____ you?
3 Please come _____ May 20th.
4 There's _____ bus _____ three thirty.
5 When _____ you want to meet _____ coffee?
6 Do you have _____ green bag?

**4** Complete the calendar with the correct words.

| | | ¹**yesterday** | today | ² _ _ _ _ _ _ _ | | Week |
|---|---|---|---|---|---|---|
| | | | | | | Month |
| | | | | | | Year |
| | ³M _ _ _ _ _ | ⁴T _ _ _ _ _ _ | ⁵W _ _ _ _ _ _ _ | ⁶T _ _ _ _ _ _ _ | ⁷F _ _ _ _ _ | the ⁸w _ _ _ _ _ _ (Saturday and ⁹S _ _ _ _ _ ) |
| 6:00 a.m.–12:00 p.m. | in the morning | | 8:00 a.m. play tennis with Marina | | | |
| 12:00 p.m.–5:00 p.m. | in the ¹⁰a _ _ _ _ _ _ _ _ | | 1:30 p.m. have lunch - Gustozo's | | | |
| 5:00 p.m.–10:00 p.m. | in the ¹¹e _ _ _ _ _ _ | | 6:00–9:00 p.m. study for exam | | | |
| 10:00 p.m.–12:00 a.m. | at ¹²n _ _ _ _ | | 10:00 p.m. call James | | | |

## GRAMMAR: Simple present (*he*, *she*, *it*)

**1** Order the words to make sentences. Write the correct capital letters.

1 **A** Ciudad Juárez / does / Gabi / in / live

_____?

**B** No, she doesn't. lives / Monterrey / in / she

_____.

2 **A** does / Lionel / study / where

_____?

**B** goes / he / the University of Chicago / to

_____.

3 **A** doesn't / have / any money / Naomi

_____.

**B** does / some today / need / she

_____?

4 **A** doesn't / your / phone / why / work

_____?

**B** I don't know. anything / do / doesn't / it

_____.

5 **A** on the weekend / does / Halcon / sports / watch

_____?

**B** Yes. he / likes watching / rugby / tennis and

_____.

**2** Complete the sentences with the verbs in the correct form of the simple present.

1 Giovanna _____ (not go) to work until 7 o'clock.

2 Alex _____ (watch) TV all day on Sundays!

3 _____ (Yannick exchange) some money before he travels?

4 This watch _____ (not work). It's very old.

5 Issam _____ (speak) to his parents every weekend.

6 Cathy is busy on Saturdays. She _____ (study) in the morning.

7 _____ (Elena exercise) much?

8 _____ (Nils want) the pasta or a pizza?

9 Her husband _____ (not like) tea or coffee.

10 _____ (you have) a car or a bike?

## VOCABULARY: Common verbs (1)

**3** Match the two parts of the sentences.

1 Do you want _____
2 I go _____
3 We live in _____
4 I don't know the _____
5 Oliver, say _____
6 On Friday evenings, we watch _____
7 I don't work _____
8 She studies _____

a answer. Do you?
b coffee or a cold drink?
c a house, not an apartment.
d to school by train.
e a movie, either a DVD or on the Internet.
f goodbye to your grandmother.
g Japanese as a hobby.
h in an office.

**4** Complete the sentences with the correct verbs.

1 Do you _____ to high school or college?

2 He doesn't want to _____ TV all day.

3 Most people _____ a computer these days.

4 My brother and sister _____ lunch for the family on weekends.

5 She doesn't _____ many sports except basketball.

6 We _____ a black-and-white cat called "Pudding."

## PRONUNCIATION: -*s* and -*es* endings

**5** ▶3.4 Put the verbs in the correct column. Then listen and check.

| changes | ~~eats~~ | goes | knows | lives |
|---------|----------|------|-------|-------|
| makes | uses | watches | works | |

| /s/ | /z/ | /ɪz/ |
|-----|-----|------|
| eats | _____ | _____ |
| _____ | _____ | _____ |
| _____ | _____ | _____ |

## WRITING: Punctuation

**1** Read the blog and choose the correct photo (a, b, or c).

 Lucía in Cádiz

| ABOUT | LATEST POST | CONTACT |

 Hello! My name's Lucía. This blog is all about my city, Cádiz in Spain.

☆ Carnival! ☆☆☆☆☆☆☆☆☆☆

It's February, and every year at this time, we celebrate Carnival, a time for singing, eating, and friends. There's lots to talk about – the singing competition,

Insert photo here

the costumes, the people, etc. – but in this post, I want to tell you about the food.

People buy food and eat it in the street. Cádiz is next to the ocean, and it is famous for its seafood: fish and other things from the ocean. In the photo, you can see *erizos*. They are ugly but I love them! But my favorite food during Carnival are the sweet cookies called *pestiños*. They're not good for you, but they're delicious!

a

b

c

**2** Rewrite the sentences with the correct punctuation and capital letters.

1 Lucía is from spain.
_____

2 Carnival's not in February.
_____

3 During Carnival, people like singing eating and seeing their friends
_____

4 people don't usually eat food in restaurants during Carnival.
_____

5 lucía thinks *erizos* are beautiful.
_____

6 Lucía's favorite food's not good for you?
_____

**3** Are the sentences in exercise 2 true or false? Write T or F.

1 ____    3 ____    5 ____
2 ____    4 ____    6 ____

**4** Match the two parts of the sentences.

1 She likes ice cream, but          ____
2 My grandfather is pretty old, but  ____
3 Sandra shops at the grocery store, but ____
4 I work in a big office and         ____
5 The festival is called New Year, but ____
6 Frida has a good job and          ____

  a he still plays sports.
  b we buy vegetables at the market.
  c I love it!
  d she's very happy.
  e it's not on January 1st.
  f her brother prefers fruit.

**5** Write a plan for a blog post about a family celebration in your house, e.g. a birthday or holiday. Answer these questions.

- When is the celebration and why do you celebrate it?
- What do you do on the day?
- What special food do you have?
- What's your favorite part of the celebration?

**6** Write your blog post. Remember to:

- use correct punctuation and capital letters.
- use the linkers *and* and *but*.

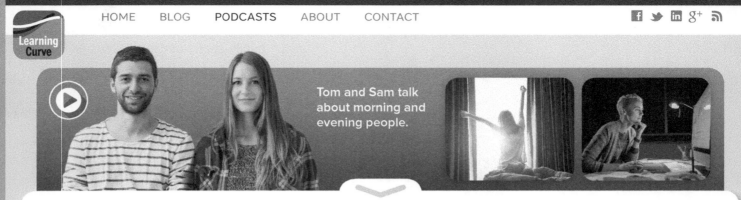

HOME    BLOG    PODCASTS    ABOUT    CONTACT

Learning Curve

Tom and Sam talk about morning and evening people.

## LISTENING

**1** ▶ 3.5 Listen to the podcast about "morning people" and "evening people." For each of the people Sam interviews (1–4), write MP (morning person), EP (evening person), or B (both).

1 _____

2 _____

3 _____

4 _____

**2** ▶ 3.5 Listen again. Complete each sentence with one word from the podcast.

1 Sam thinks Tom is an _____ person.

2 Sam asked four different people the _____ question yesterday.

3 Speaker 1 is an _____.

4 Speaker 1 works every _____.

5 Speaker 2 is a _____.

6 Speaker 2's _____ sleep in the morning.

7 Speaker 3 works in a _____.

8 Speaker 3 sometimes sleeps in a quiet _____.

9 Speaker 4 works during the _____.

10 Speaker 4 says _____ are expensive at night.

## READING

**1** Read Jack's blog about cooking. Match paragraphs 1–4 with photos a–d.

1 _____

2 _____

3 _____

4 _____

**2** Read the blog again. Choose the correct answers.

1 The food Jack likes is _____.
 a expensive and difficult to cook
 b expensive and easy to cook
 c cheap and easy to cook

2 Jack says people can _____ for quick recipes.
 a look in a book
 b look on the Internet
 c ask a chef

3 Jack says a simple pasta dish can take _____ to cook.
 a ten minutes
 b 30 minutes
 c three hours

4 Jack says chefs _____ learning to cook.
 a don't spend a long time
 b spend a long time
 c don't like

5 Jack says _____ aren't expensive.
 a meat and fish
 b vegetables
 c pasta and tomatoes

6 Jack thinks the best thing people can do is _____.
 a buy food from a store
 b buy food from other countries
 c grow their own food

7 Jack says food that _____ can be bad for the planet.
 a is expensive
 b comes from other countries
 c is difficult to cook

HOME BLOG PODCASTS ABOUT CONTACT

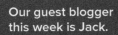

Our guest blogger this week is Jack.

# KEEP IT simple

Many people think all the best meals are very expensive and difficult to cook. But it's just not true! Most of my favorite dishes are very easy to make, and cheap, too! Let's look at four ways to make cooking cheap and easy, and why it's important.

Grown your own!

**1** It's true that many of the most famous dishes in good restaurants take a long time to cook. In fact, sometimes chefs start a meal days before they serve it! But most people don't have three hours to cook a meal every evening. The good news is there are hundreds of quick recipes online – meals that take less than 30 minutes from start to finish. For a very quick meal, a plate of pasta and tomato sauce only takes ten minutes!

Think local!

**2** Chefs study how to cook for years, and we can do a lot of different things in the kitchen. But some of my favorite dishes are very, very simple. A piece of fish with some fresh vegetables is delicious, and really easy to cook. Because it only uses a few ingredients, the taste is clean and fresh.

Simple to make!

**3** In many restaurants, you spend a lot of money to have a nice meal. But good food isn't always expensive. In most countries, good meat and fish is expensive, but vegetables are cheap. And food from other countries often costs a lot of money. It's better to buy food from your own country. Or even better, grow your own food!

Start early!

**4** Cheap, simple, local food is good for you and it's good for the planet. Food from other countries often travels hundreds of miles by airplane. This is bad for everyone. That's another reason to use food from near where you live.

Go to my website for lots of cheap and easy recipes. Or come to my restaurant and let me cook for you!

## GRAMMAR: Frequency adverbs

**1** Choose the correct place in each sentence for the adverb in parentheses: (a), (b), or (c).

1  I (a) have (b) lunch (c) at 1 o'clock. (*usually*)
2  (a) He (b) drinks hot milk (c). (*never*)
3  That store (a) has (b) expensive sunglasses (c) and cheap ones. (*often*)
4  We (a) watch (b) a movie on Friday night (c). (*always*)
5  My sister and I (a) do (b) our homework (c) together. (*sometimes*)
6  Engineers (a) use (b) a computer (c) all day. (*often*)
7  (a) They (b) leave class (c) early. (*never*)
8  (a) Marco (b) comes (c) late to work! (*always*)

**2** Look at the calendar. Then complete the sentences about Shruthi's day. Use adverbs of frequency.

| Monday | Tuesday | Wednesday | Thursday | Friday |
| --- | --- | --- | --- | --- |
| 6:30 a.m. play sports | 6:30 a.m. play sports | 6:30 a.m. play sports | 6:45 a.m. play sports | 6:30 a.m. play sports |
| 7:45 a.m. have breakfast with Ana | 7:45 a.m. have breakfast with Ana | 7.45 a.m. have breakfast with Ana | | 7:45 a.m. have breakfast with Ana |
| 8:30–6.00 work | 8:30–6:30 work | 8.30–6.00 work | 8:30–6:30 work | 8:30–6:00 work |
| | 1:00 p.m. go to Mario's restaurant | | 1:30 p.m. go to Brown's restaurant | 1:00 p.m. go to El Toro restaurant |
| 6:00 p.m. leave work | 6:30 p.m. leave work | 6:00 p.m. leave work | 6:30 p.m. leave work | 6:00 p.m. leave work |
| 6:30 p.m. study Japanese | 7:00 p.m. study Japanese | | 7:00 p.m. study Japanese | |
| 7:30 p.m. watch TV | 9:30 p.m. watch TV | 8:45 p.m. watch TV | 9:00 p.m. watch TV | 8:00 p.m. see movie at the movie theater |

1  Shruthi  *always plays sports*  before 7:00 a.m.
2  She _____ breakfast with Ana.
3  She _____ from eight thirty.
4  She _____ to a restaurant for lunch.
5  She _____ work before 6:00 p.m.
6  She _____ studies Japanese after work.
7  She _____ a movie at the movie theater.
8  She _____ TV in the evenings.

## VOCABULARY: Daily routine verbs

**3** Order the letters to make daily routine verbs.

I'm a chef, so I have a long day. I [1] *teg pu* _____ at seven o'clock and wake my children up. After I [2] *teg ddeerss* _____, I make breakfast. Mornings are the only time I see the children. We [3] *aeelv ehmo* _____ at eight thirty – I don't [4] *arstt korw* _____ until eleven, but I take the children to school before that. My job is difficult and I don't [5] *fiihns krow* _____ until eleven o'clock! I always [6] *ekta a ehrosw* _____ before I [7] *og ot bde* _____ at night.

**4** Look at the pictures. Complete the sentences with daily routine verbs.

1  She _____ to music when she's on the bus.

2  I usually _____ in the mornings.

3  We _____ together in our bedroom.

4  He _____ late in the evening.

5  They _____ at the mall every Sunday.

6  Do you _____ when you go to bed?

## PRONUNCIATION: Sentence stress

**5** ▶ 4.1  Listen to the sentences. Pay attention to the sentence stress. Listen again and repeat.

1  I never have breakfast at a café.
2  He sometimes studies on the weekend.
3  It's often cold here at night.
4  They usually eat salad with lunch.
5  We always watch TV on the computer.
6  She never says "thank you."

## READING: Finding specific information

**1** Complete the sentences with transportation words.

1 This is another word for *underground train* or *metro*. _____

2 This goes very fast, like a car, but has two wheels. _____

3 This is like a boat, goes on water, and is usually very big. _____

4 You can pay someone to drive you in this car. _____

5 This is big and lots of people pay to go to work on the road in it. _____

6 This has two wheels and you can ride it for exercise. _____

7 You can travel by air to other countries in this. _____

8 This is big, it doesn't go on the road, and you pay to travel in it. _____

**2** Read the article about five people's trips. Match each person with the correct transportation. You can use more than one letter.

1 Giovanna _____    a bike
2 Jiang _____    b bus
3 Lupita _____    c ferry
4 Gary _____    d on foot
5 Henry _____    e plane
                    f the subway

**3** Read the article again. Choose the correct options to complete the sentences. Where in the text is the information?

1 The article is about people's *favorite / difficult / daily* trips.

2 The *vaporetto* is a *plane / ferry / train*.

3 Jiang travels for *30 minutes / two and a half hours / five hours* every day.

4 It's difficult for Lupita to *study at home / go to school / get home*.

5 In some parts of Australia, doctors travel by *boat / motorbike / plane*.

6 Henry goes by bike because it is *cheap / clean / fast*.

**4** Complete the sentences with a person's name or a place from the article. Then choose P for possession or C for contraction.

1 _____'s Australian.    P   C

2 Singapore, _____'s city, is perfect for bikes.    P   C

3 _____'s job is in Venice.    P   C

4 _____'s a high school student.    P   C

5 The college in Nanjing is not near _____'s home.    P   C

6 Giovanna uses _____'s public transportation.    P   C

**Giovanna** is a tour guide in Venice, Italy. Like many people, she travels around by *vaporetto*, the local "bus" service... except in Venice, these buses don't go on the road, they are ferries! "I love my trip to work," she says.

**Jiang** studies in Nanjing, China. His college is a long way from home. He takes two buses, the subway, and then walks for 30 minutes. The total time for his trip? Two and a half hours each way!

**Lupita's** house is in the mountains in Colombia, but her high school is a long way down the mountain. She goes on foot. "Going to school is easy," she says, "but getting home is very difficult!"

It's not always easy to get to the place you want. Many people study or work far from their homes. Here are five people with interesting daily trips.

**Gary** is one of Australia's "flying doctors." He often travels long distances to see his patients, sometimes hundreds of miles. How? By plane!

**Henry** gets everywhere really fast in his city, Singapore. "This is the perfect city to use a bike," he says. "It's so safe and easy."

## GRAMMAR: Simple present: *wh-* questions

**1** Match questions 1–9 with answers a–i. Then complete the questions with the words in the box.

> how    ~~how many~~    how old    what
> what time    when    where    who    why

1   _How many_   brothers and sisters do you have?   _e_
2   _____ do people here do on weekends?    ____
3   _____ is Greta happy?    ____
4   _____ does the class start?    ____
5   _____ is he?    ____
6   _____ do your parents live?    ____
7   _____ is that girl on the TV?    ____
8   _____ do they get to work?    ____
9   _____ is her birthday?    ____

a   At 9:45, I think.
b   They go on the subway.
c   It's next Tuesday.
d   She's a singer.
e   ~~I have two sisters.~~
f   In a beautiful place called Puebla.
g   Most people go to the beach.
h   He's three today!
i   Because she has a new job.

**2** Order the words to make questions. Add *do*, *does*, *am*, *is*, or *are*.

1   movie / what / your favorite
_____?

2   how / know / the answer / they
_____?

3   by car / Casey / go / to school / why
_____?

4   old / your mother / how
_____?

5   finish / Jerry / time / what / work
_____?

6   glasses / my / where
_____?

7   how / you live / many / people / with
_____?

8   the teacher / this / morning / where
_____?

9   get / home / when / your / brother
_____?

10   in the class / know / who / you
_____?

## VOCABULARY: Adjectives (2)

**3** ▶ 4.2 Complete the conversations with a pair of words in the box in the correct order. Listen and check.

> clean/dirty    cold/hot    long/short
> horrible/nice    noisy/quiet

1   **A** Is it _____ in here?
   **B** No, it's only 55 °F. I'm pretty _____.
2   **A** You're very _____! I want to listen to the radio.
   **B** I'm sorry, Mom. I'll be _____.
3   **A** I don't want to watch a _____ movie. It's late.
   **B** OK. This movie is very _____ – only 80 minutes.
4   **A** Is the city _____?
   **B** No! It's _____. I don't like the noise and the traffic!
5   **A** I'm very _____ from doing housework.
   **B** Yes, now the house is _____, but you're not! Take a shower!

**4** Complete each sentence with the correct adjective.

1   Buy a s __ __ __ __ cake, not a big one, because not many people know about the party.
2   I love Mexico. It's interesting and the people are very f __ __ __ __ __ __ __.
3   It takes six hours to get to the city on the s __ __ __ train, but the tickets are cheap.
4   New electric cars are quiet and they are also f __ __ __.
5   Our hotel room is fantastic. It has a really l __ __ __ __ bed.
6   We never go to that grocery store – the salesclerks are so u __ __ __ __ __ __ __ __ __!

## PRONUNCIATION: Question words

**5** ▶ 4.3 Listen to the questions. Are *do* and *does* stressed? Listen again, check, and repeat.

1   When do you listen to the radio?
2   What books does he read?
3   How many movies do they watch each week?
4   Who does she go to the movies with?
5   Why do you like shopping?
6   What time do you study?

## SPEAKING: Shopping for food

**1** ▶ 4.4 Look at the pictures and listen to a customer in a store. Does the customer buy a, b, or c?

**a**

**b**

**c**

**2** ▶ 4.4 Choose the correct options to complete the conversation. Then listen again and check.

1 How _____ I help you?
   **a** do          **b** can          **c** am

2 Do _____ have fruit juice?
   **a** you         **b** I            **c** we

3 _____ I have orange juice, please?
   **a** Do          **b** Am           **c** Can

4 How _____ is that?
   **a** much        **b** many         **c** more

5 I'd _____ some of that, please.
   **a** want        **b** like         **c** have

6 Here you are. _____ else?
   **a** Nothing     **b** Something    **c** Anything

7 _____ thirteen dollars and twenty-five cents.
   **a** That's      **b** This is      **c** Here's

8 Here _____ go.
   **a** I           **b** you          **c** they

9 And _____ your change.
   **a** it's        **b** here's       **c** where's

**3** ▶ 4.5 Look at the photos and listen to three conversations. Match the conversations (1–3) with the photos (a–c).

1 _____   2 _____   3 _____

**a**

**b**

$199⁹⁹

**c**

**4** ▶ 4.5 Listen to the three conversations again. Write 1, 2, or 3.

**a** The customer and the salesclerk are polite. _____

**b** The customer is <u>not</u> polite. _____

**c** The salesclerk is <u>not</u> polite. _____

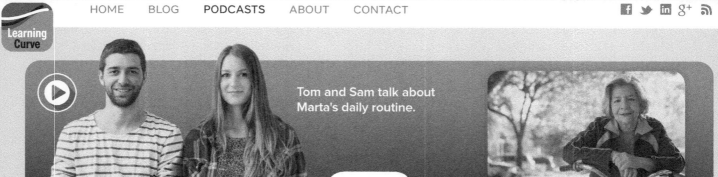

HOME    BLOG    PODCASTS    ABOUT    CONTACT

Tom and Sam talk about Marta's daily routine.

## LISTENING

**1** ▶ **4.6** Listen to the podcast about a person's daily routine. Check (✔) the verbs you hear.

a  get up            _____

b  take a shower     _____

c  get dressed       _____

d  have breakfast    _____

e  do housework      _____

f  leave home        _____

g  start work        _____

h  finish work       _____

i  get home          _____

j  do homework       _____

**2** ▶ **4.6** Listen again and choose the correct answers.

1  Where is Marta from?
   a  France
   b  Brazil
   c  Spain

2  What time does Marta's day start?
   a  5:00
   b  5:15
   c  5:30

3  How does Marta travel to her daughter's house?
   a  on the subway
   b  by bike
   c  by car

4  How far is Marta's house from her daughter's house?
   a  five miles
   b  ten miles
   c  fifteen miles

5  What time does Marta's daughter arrive home?
   a  6:00
   b  6:30
   c  8:30

6  What does Marta do before she goes to bed?
   a  She cooks a meal.
   b  She watches TV.
   c  She reads a book.

## READING

**1** Read Penny's blog about a long trip. How many types of transportation does José tell her about?

a  eight

b  nine

c  ten

**2** Read the blog again. Write Y (Yes) or N (No).

1  Penny's family doesn't like her travel plans. _____

2  José is Chilean.                              _____

3  The bus from Lima to Cusco is expensive.      _____

4  The trip to Machu Picchu by car is easy.      _____

5  Most people go to La Paz by bike.             _____

6  José thinks the people in La Paz are nice.    _____

7  Walking tours in Santiago are cheap.          _____

8  Buenos Aires is a good city to see on foot.   _____

**3** Match the adjectives with their opposites.

1  cold     _____     a  unfriendly

2  noisy    _____     b  quiet

3  fast     _____     c  horrible

4  friendly _____     d  cold

5  long     _____     e  hot

6  nice     _____     f  dirty

7  clean    _____     g  slow

8  hot      _____     h  short

HOME  **BLOG**  PODCASTS  ABOUT  CONTACT

Guest blogger Penny tells us about her latest travel plans.

# A long trip

"It's a very bad idea." That's what everyone says when I tell them my travel plans. And this is what my friends and family say when I tell them my new idea – to spend one month traveling from Lima in Peru to Buenos Aires in Argentina. "It's dangerous!" says my mother. "It's expensive!" says my father. "It's really hot!" says one friend. "It's really cold!" says another friend. Maybe they're right, but there is one thing I know – it's going to be an exciting trip!

It's a long trip and I don't want to be in a bus or car for a month. My plan is to use different types of transportation on my trip. My friend José is from Mexico, but he knows Peru and Chile very well. So, I asked him for help and he sent me this information. Thanks José!

OK, Penny, you start your adventure in Lima. It's about seven hours from New York by plane. From Lima you go to the town of Cusco by bus. The bus is noisy and it's not fast, but it's cheap. And there are beds! Cusco is famous because it's near Machu Picchu. The best way to get to Machu Picchu from Cusco is by train and then on foot. It is possible to go by car but don't – the roads are very bad! After Machu Picchu, take the train back to Cusco and your next stop is La Paz, in Bolivia.

Most people travel to La Paz by bus, but why don't you go by bike? You go around the beautiful Lake Titicaca. Stop for a day and see the lake by boat – it's an amazing place! Seven more days on your bike and you arrive in La Paz. Spend two or three days in La Paz because it's a very interesting city with friendly people.

I have an idea for the trip to Santiago in Chile – go by motorcycle! It's a long trip (about four days), but the views are great. Santiago is another interesting city, and the best way to see it is on foot. There are walking tours and they're not expensive.

Your final trip is by train from Santiago to Buenos Aires. It's a long trip so go to the city of Mendoza by bus. Then take a different bus to Buenos Aires. The buses in Chile and Argentina are cheap and clean. Buenos Aires is a great city, but it is very big to see on foot. Travel on the subway to see everything.

What an exciting trip. Have fun!

# All about me

**5A** — **LANGUAGE**

## GRAMMAR: *can* and *can't*

**1** Complete the sentences and questions with *can*, *can't*, and the verbs in the box.

| take | eat | read | start | study | ~~watch~~ |

1 A _____*Can*_____ we ____*watch*____ a movie?

   B No, you ___*can't*___!

2 A I _____ _____ work at seven a.m. No problem.

   B That's great!

3 A _____ I _____ a shower?

   B Yes, you _____!

4 A He's only three, but he _____ _____ books.

   B That's amazing!

5 A What's the problem?

   B It's very noisy! I _____ _____ in here!

6 A _____ your dog _____ chocolate?

   B No, he _____, it's bad for him.

**2** Complete the conversations. Use *can* or *can't* and any other words you need.

1 "It's my brother's birthday tomorrow." "Really? I _____ a cake for him!"

2 "Can you speak Russian, Dominic?" "Yes, _____. Why? Is that an e-mail from your Russian friend?"

3 "Emma says she knows about computers, but she _____ her new tablet." "I'm sure she _____. We _____ help her. It's easy!"

4 "We have some dollars, but we need euros in Paris. _____ some money at that bank?" "No, _____. The bank's not open today."

5 "My grandfather is very old, but he _____ a newspaper without glasses." "_____ a car without them?"

6 "Can Sheila go shopping today?" "No, _____."

## VOCABULARY: Common verbs (2)

**3** Choose the correct verbs to complete the sentences.

I [1] *call / speak / travel* my grandmother every day, but on Wednesdays and Fridays, I go to her house to [2] *arrive / give / look after* her because she can't [3] *cook / give / help* her own lunch. Sometimes my sister [4] *speaks / helps / calls* me, but I usually do it alone. My grandmother sometimes [5] *dances / plays / sings* the piano for me. She also likes to get out of the house, so I often [6] *drive / arrive / travel* her to the ocean. She loves to [7] *call / travel / swim* in the ocean. On weekends, she sometimes [8] *helps / meets / sings* her friends for coffee.

**4** Complete each pair of sentences with the same verb in the correct form.

1 A You must _____ at the airport two hours before your flight.

   B He always _____ late.

2 A She doesn't _____ salsa, but she's good at ballet.

   B I love this band! Do you want to _____ with me?

3 A My French isn't very good, but I can _____ Spanish.

   B Do you often _____ to your brothers?

4 A I _____ to different countries for my job.

   B It's easy to _____ to the city by train.

5 A Do the students _____ presents to their teachers?

   B He never _____ me back my pen after class!

6 A I can't _____, but I love listening to music.

   B It's a very difficult song to _____.

7 A The ocean's too cold to _____ in today.

   B I sometimes _____ in the pool in town.

## PRONUNCIATION: *can* and *can't*

**5** ▶5.1 Listen to the sentences. Write affirmative (+), negative (−), or question (?). Listen again, check, and repeat.

1 _____        5 _____

2 _____        6 _____

3 _____        7 _____

4 _____        8 _____

# LISTENING: Listening for specific information

**1** Match sentences 1–6 with the pairs of photos a–f. Then complete the words with the missing vowels (a, e, i, o, u).

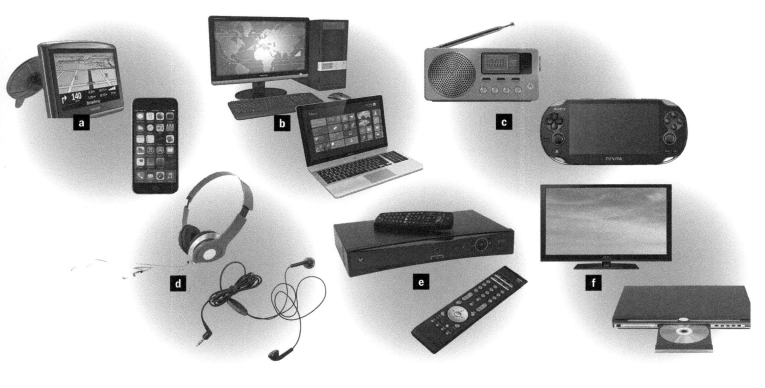

1 I don't have a d___skt___p  c___mp___t___r. I have a l___pt___p.

2 Many people watch movies on t___l___v___s___n from the Internet but some also have DVD pl___y___rs.

3 I can't use ___ ___rph___n___s, so I use h___ ___dph___n___s to listen to music.

4 There's no need for a GPS in your car if you own a sm___rtph___n___.

5 I play v___d___ ___g___m___s or listen to the r___d___ ___ on the bus.

6 This r___m___t___  c___ntr___l is for the DVR – the "d___g___t___l  v___d___ ___  r___c___rd___r."

**2** ⊳ **5.2** Listen to a radio show about technology. Choose the best title, a, b, or c.

a Three reasons why people don't use technology.

b Three electronic devices people use.

c Three people with technology problems.

**3** Read the sentences. Are the missing words a person, place, number, or thing?

1 The speaker uses electronic technology for about ___*number*___ hours each day.

2 The speaker's _____ doesn't need a cell phone.

3 A family can use the Internet in _____ or more ways, with different electronic devices.

4 Some people think that the _____ is not safe.

5 They think that big Internet companies want our personal _____.

6 People in the _____ look at screens for about twelve hours every day.

**4** ⊳ **5.2** Listen again and complete the sentences in exercise 3.

**5** ⊳ **5.3** Read the sentences and underline the important words. Then listen, check, and repeat.

1 My family comes from China, but I live in Japan.

2 I can't buy the black laptop because it's too expensive.

3 That tablet is my sister's, not mine.

4 I study Spanish, so I listen to Spanish radio online.

**6** ⊳ **5.4** Listen and write the important words.

1 I usually _____ _____ on my _____ before I _____ to _____.

2 Craig _____ _____ to _____ in his _____.

3 It says on the _____ that the _____ _____ at _____ o'clock.

## GRAMMAR: Object pronouns

**1** Choose the correct pronouns to complete the text.

Hi! My name's Gabriela, but I don't like ¹ *her / it / she*, so people call me Gabi. I'm 20 years old, and I'm a college student. There are lots of young people there, but I'm not like most of ² *him / them / they*. They like dancing and enjoying themselves in the evening, but those things aren't fun for ³ *it / me / them*. I love sports, and I play ⁴ *them / they / us* with my friends, Piotr and Maggie. Piotr enjoys going out on his bike, so I often go bike riding with ⁵ *he / her / him*. Maggie loves swimming, so I go with ⁶ *her / it / she* to the swimming pool every Tuesday. Why do we like exercising? Because it's good for ⁷ *it / us / we*, and we're happy when we do ⁸ *it / them / him*. What about ⁹ *her / us / you*? Do you enjoy sports or do you hate ¹⁰ *him / them / me*?

**2** Complete each sentence with one object pronoun and one subject pronoun.

1 Can I have your pen? I only need _____ for a minute. Oh, no, _____'s red! I need a black one.

2 _____ don't speak Portuguese well, but my friend João teaches _____ every week.

3 Evgeny and I like the same music. _____ normally listen to rap and R&B. Katerina likes the same music as _____.

4 Excuse me, are _____ OK? Can I help _____?

5 I go to the gym with Jamie. _____ takes me in her car. It's very nice of _____.

6 Lali and Naomi don't like the beach. It's too hot for _____ and _____ can't swim.

7 Michel studies English with me. _____'s from Vietnam. I often see _____ after school.

8 Patricia is an actress. I sometimes see _____ on television, but _____'s not very famous.

## VOCABULARY: Activities

**3** ▶5.5 Listen and write the activities.

| Jobs in the house | Sports |
|---|---|
| 1 _____ | 3 _____ |
| 2 _____ | 4 _____ |

| Evenings and weekends | Activities on your own |
|---|---|
| 5 _____ | 7 _____ |
| 6 _____ | _____ |
| _____ | 8 _____ |

**4** Complete each sentence with an activity.

1 She loves _____, but she doesn't have a bike!

2 _____ magazines is a great way to learn a new language.

3 There's no food in the house. We need to do some _____ _____ today.

4 _____ in the ocean is very cold in some _____ _____ countries!

5 I don't enjoy _____ at the movie theater, but I like them on TV.

6 They're not good at _____ to disco music, but they like watching other people do it.

## PRONUNCIATION: /h/

**5** ▶5.6 Listen. Pay attention to the sound /h/. Listen again and repeat.

1 A How's your homework?
  B It's hard!

2 A He has lots of housework.
  B Doesn't Hillary help?

3 A Is her husband happy?
  B No, he hates his job.

4 A Hello. How is your vacation?
  B It's very hot!

5 A Are those his headphones?
  B No, they're Heidi's.

6 A When does Harry leave home?
  B At eight thirty.

## WRITING: Describing yourself

**1** Read Margarita's profile. Which questions (1–7) does it answer? Write the paragraphs (a–d).

1 How do you travel around the city? ____
2 Where do you live? ____
3 What do you like doing in your free time? ____
4 What do you like watching on TV? ____
5 What job do you do? ____
6 What do you like to eat? ____
7 What jobs does your family do? ____

# About me

**a** Hi! My name's Margarita, but you can call me Marga. I'm a police officer. It's an interesting job ¹ ____.

**b** I live in Recife, a city in the north of Brazil. Many tourists visit Recife ² ____. I live downtown in an apartment with my friend Camila.

**c** In my free time I like reading and cooking. I go running, but I don't like it much ³ ____. But I love swimming. Recife has a great beach, so I go there two or three times a week.

**d** My family is from Recife. They live near me. I have two brothers and a little sister. My sister is in college. She studies IT ⁴ ____. My father and one of my brothers are police officers, like me. My other brother is a really good chef in an expensive restaurant, but he doesn't do the cooking when we are all together at home ⁵ ____!

**2** Match reasons a–g with blanks 1–5 in the profile. There are two extra reasons.

a because he thinks home cooking is too easy ____
b because I meet lots of different people and help them with their problems ____
c because the people are unfriendly ____
d because it's boring ____
e because she wants to be a computer programmer ____
f because I can't drive ____
g because it's a beautiful place near the ocean ____

**3** Write a personal profile for someone in your family, a friend, or a famous person. Make sure you:

- answer some of the questions in exercise 1.
- use paragraphs.
- give reasons with *because*.

HOME    BLOG    PODCASTS    ABOUT    CONTACT

Learning Curve

Tom and Sam talk to four people about things they can't do.

## LISTENING

**1** ▶ 5.7 Listen to the podcast about things people can't do. Complete each sentence with one or two words.

1 Lorenzo can't _____.

2 Beatrice can't _____.

3 Zoe can't _____.

4 Roberto can't _____.

**2** ▶ 5.7 Listen again. Choose T (true) or F (false).

| | |
|---|---|
| 1 Sam thinks she can cook. | T / F |
| 2 Lorenzo doesn't have a car. | T / F |
| 3 Lorenzo's friends never go to the beach. | T / F |
| 4 Beatrice can't dance. | T / F |
| 5 Zoe's daughter can swim. | T / F |
| 6 Zoe wants to learn how to swim. | T / F |
| 7 Roberto can speak Spanish. | T / F |
| 8 Roberto wants a Portuguese teacher. | T / F |

**3** Write the common verbs.

1 Can you p_____ any musical instruments?

2 Let's m_____ this afternoon outside school.

3 I can dance well, but I can't s_____ at all!

4 When you get home this evening, c_____ me.

5 Which countries do you want to t_____ to in the future?

6 I sometimes l_____ a_____ my grandparents' dog.

7 Please h_____ me to carry these bags into the house.

8 What time does the bus a_____ downtown?

## READING

**1** Read Marc's blog about technology. Match the best title with blanks 1–3.

a Do we use smartphones differently?

b Do we use different kinds of technology?

c Do we spend different amounts of time online?

**2** Read the blog again. Choose the correct words to complete the sentences.

1 The survey says old and young people are _____.
a the same
b different
c both the same and different

2 _____ of older people own an MP3 player.
a 26%
b 60%
c 74%

3 People of different ages all use _____.
a headphones
b desktop computers
c the Internet

4 Marc's grandmother _____ every evening.
a listens to the radio
b watches TV
c goes online

5 Old and young people use their smartphones to _____.
a take photos
b make calls
c watch videos

6 Marc thinks older people play games because _____.
a they have money
b they don't work
c the games are free

HOME    BLOG    PODCASTS    ABOUT    CONTACT

Our guest blogger Marc looks at the different ways young and old people use technology.

# Technology
## for the
## **young** and **old**

How old are you? What technology do you have? What do you use it for? How often do you use it? A new survey in the U.S. asks people these questions, and here are some of the results.

## 1 _____

Can you guess the answer to this question: Which group has more desktop computers: people aged 18–34 or people aged 57–65? The answer is interesting – it's the older group. Can you guess why? It's because young people have laptops and smartphones. They don't need desktop computers!  Another interesting result of the survey is about music. Only 26% of people aged 60 and above have an MP3 player. For people in their twenties it's 74%. But does this mean old people don't listen to music? Of course not! My parents often listen to music, but they do it at home. And they like the same music, so they never need headphones!

## 2 _____

The survey says that almost all ages use the Internet. I think that's interesting because some people think that the Internet is only for young people. In fact, only very old people don't go online. But young people do spend more time online than older people. This doesn't surprise me – most of my friends spend hours on the Internet every day. A lot of us need it for our jobs. But I think old people spend a lot of time using other technology. My grandmother is nearly 80. It's true that she never goes online – she doesn't even have a computer! But she loves listening to the radio and she watches TV for hours every evening. She's very fast with the remote control!

## 3 _____

One fact from the survey is that most older people only use their smartphones for one or two things. But young people make calls, send messages, go online, buy things, listen to music, and watch videos – all on their smartphones. Both age groups use their smartphones to take photos, but the type of photos is different. Young people love to take selfies! Another fact from the survey was about social media. Old people use it to find old friends and chat with their families. Young people use social media to find new friends. But my favorite fact from the survey was this: it says that old people play a lot of free games online! I think I know why this is – they don't have jobs. It's easy to play games when you have a lot of time!

## WRITING: Filling out a form

**1** ▶ WP1   Listen to the conversation at a bus station. Fill out the 'lost and found' form.

| Greyford Bus Services | Personal details |
|---|---|
| Title: Mr. [ ✓ ]   Mrs. [ ]   Ms. [ ] | |
| First name: *Anthony* | Last name: ¹_____ |
| Street address: ²_____ *Maple Street* | E-mail address:<br>⁴_____@starmail.com |
| City, State: ³_____, *Massachusetts* | Phone number: *617-231-3327* |
| Zip code: *02445* | Date of birth (MM/DD/YYYY):<br>*03/15/* ⁵_____ |
| **Details of lost item** | |
| Object: *brown wallet with $40 and credit card* | |
| Date lost: *02/13/2018 at about 9:30 a.m.* | |
| Place lost: *bus number* ⁶_____ | |

**2** ▶ WP2   Listen to another conversation and correct five pieces of information.

| Greyford Bus Services | Personal details |
|---|---|
| Title: Mr. [ ]   Mrs. [ ✓ ]   Ms. [ ] | |
| First name: *Nithya* | Last name: *Patil* |
| Street address: *5573 Sycamore Drive* | E-mail address: *nithya@padmail.com* |
| City, State: *Austin, Texas* | Phone number: *512-527-6906* |
| Zip code: *79759* | Date of birth (MM/DD/YYYY): *02/01/1989* |

**3** Write the sentences again with capital letters where you need them.

1  he's in the u.s. but he's japanese.

_____

2  i am from rouen, in france.

_____

3  my zip code is 78759.

_____

4  his sister speaks chinese and french.

_____

5  these are michael's keys.

_____

6  she lives at 6 green street.

_____

**4** Complete Michi's form with the information in the box. Use capital letters where you need them.

> 305-555-9846   mrs. fujioka   08/31/1981   miami   40 park street
> 33166   japanese   m_fujioka@starmail.com   michi

| Personal details | | | |
|---|---|---|---|
| Title | ¹_____ | Zip code | ⁶_____ |
| First name | ²_____ | E-mail address | ⁷_____ |
| Last name | ³_____ | Phone number | ⁸_____ |
| Street address | ⁴_____ | Nationality | ⁹_____ |
| Town/City | ⁵_____ | Date of birth (MM/DD/YYYY)<br>¹⁰_____ | |

## WRITING: Punctuation

**1** Read the blog post about three men's trips to work or school. Match the names with the reasons they travel so far (a–c). Don't look at blanks 1–5.

| | | |
|---|---|---|
| **1** Joshua | ____ | **a** His family lives far from where he works/studies. |
| **2** David | ____ | **b** He doesn't have the money to live near where he works/studies. |
| **3** Pat | ____ | **c** He doesn't want to live near where he works/studies. |

---

# Stories of daily commutes*

I'm Joshua. ¹_____ In fact, it takes me over an hour and fifteen minutes to get to work. ²_____ I do it because the good jobs are in the city, but it's expensive to live there. But why do other people commute long distances?

David Givens has one of the longest commutes in the United States – 600 kilometers a day from the mountains in Mariposa County to San José, California. It's a long trip, three and a half hours each way, but David says it's great because his life in Mariposa is so wonderful, and he prefers it to San José. ³_____

Pat Skinner leaves home at seven to drive 80 kilometers. ⁴_____ But Pat's not an office worker commuting to work; he's an eleven-year-old schoolboy. His mom drives him about 500 kilometers each week so that he can go to a good private school. He does his homework in the car!

How far do you commute each day? ⁵_____ Comment below!

**\*commute – (n and v) trip to work every day**

---

**2** Add the punctuation to these sentences. Then match them with blanks 1–5 in the blog in exercise 1.

**a** at seven in the evening he gets home

**b** davids house is in the mountains its a clean place far from the cities of the coast

**c** do you like your trip to work

**d** every morning, i ride my bike to the station and get on a busy train into the city

**e** I work in london and, like many people, i spend a lot of my day between home and work

**3** Complete the sentences with *and* or *but*.

**1** He usually rides his bike, _____ today he's on the bus.

**2** Why does Andy walk to work _____ take the train home?

**3** Every morning, Breana buys a coffee _____ a cookie at the station.

**4** I live _____ work in the same town, so I don't travel far every day.

**5** My mother's office is in the city, _____ on Fridays she works at home.

**6** They work in the same office _____ go to work together.

**4** You are going to write a blog post about a trip you often make (every day/week/month). Use these questions to plan your writing.

- Where do you go?
- How far is the trip (minutes and hours or kilometers)?
- How do you travel?
- Do you enjoy it? Why/Why not?
- Do you travel with other people?
- What do you see on the trip?
- Is the trip expensive/interesting/difficult, etc.?

**5** Write your blog post.

- Use correct punctuation and capital letters correctly.
- Use the linkers *and* and *but*.

## WRITING: Describing yourself

**1** Read Olga's personal profile. Then match questions a–f with paragraphs 1–4. There are two extra questions.

a  What are you good at?  _____

b  What are your hobbies?  _____

c  What's your family like?  _____

d  What's your plan in the next five years?  _____

e  Where do you live and what's it like?  _____

f  Who are you and what do you do?  _____

● ○ ○

# LET'S LEARN A LANGUAGE!

**Olga** St. Petersburg

**1**  Hi everyone. I'm Olga from Russia. I'm nineteen. Right now, I'm a student in college. I'm studying teaching, and I plan to teach languages one day.

**2**  I'm from Yekaterinburg, but I study in St. Petersburg, Russia's second city. I don't have my own apartment – this city is very expensive – but I share a big apartment with four other students. It's near to the college, the park, and a large shopping mall. St. Petersburg is a beautiful city for nine months of the year, but it can get very cold and dark around January!

**3**  In my spare time, I enjoy reading, listening to music, and learning languages – I speak three already and my Portuguese is OK. Why do I want to improve my English? Because it lets me speak to the world and because I need it if I want to work in a good school.

**4**  I don't see my family very often because I live so far from home. I have an older brother – he works as a doctor in Yekaterinburg, and he has two lovely children. My younger brother is at school and lives with my parents. My dad is an engineer and my mom is a journalist. She works at home.

**2** Read the profile again. Write T (true) or F (false).

1  Olga has a job in a school.  _____

2  She doesn't live in her home city.  _____

3  Five people live in her apartment.  _____

4  St. Petersburg is a lovely place to live all year.  _____

5  She only learns languages because she wants to.  _____

6  She has two brothers.  _____

7  Her mother is a doctor.  _____

8  The website is for people who want to learn languages.  _____

**3** Use the prompts to write sentences with *because*.

1  Abbey / never / go / dancing / very expensive

_____.

2  I / not need / a car / there / stores / near / our house

_____.

3  Jamie / love / weekends / he / sleep / late

_____!

4  Why / she / do / yoga / ? / want / make friends

_____

5  I / can / run / today / have / bad knee

_____

6  Why / I / like / this movie theater / ? / cheap

_____!

**4** Write a personal profile for a language exchange website.

• Use paragraphs.

• Say the language(s) you speak and the language(s) you want to practice.

• Give reasons with *because*.

## Richmond

58 St Aldates
Oxford
OX1 1ST
United Kingdom

**Eighth reprint:** 2023
**ISBN:** 978-84-668-2888-8
**CP:** 880334
© Richmond / Santillana Global S.L. 2018

**Publishing Director:** Deborah Tricker

**Publisher:** Simone Foster

**Media Publisher:** Sue Ashcroft

**Workbook Publisher:** Luke Baxte

**Content Developer:** David Cole-Powney

**Editors:** Sue Jones, Debra Emmett, Tom Hadland, Fiona Hunt, Laura Miranda, Helen Wendholt

**Proofreaders:** Pippa Mayfield, Shannon Niell, Jamie Bowman, Amanda Leigh

**Design Manager:** Lorna Heaslip

**Cover Design:** This Ain't Rock'n'Roll, London

**Design & Layout:** Lorna Heaslip, Dave Kuzmicki, emc design Ltd.

**Photo Researcher:** Magdalena Mayo

***Learning Curve* video:** Mannic Media

**Audio production:** John Marshall Media

**App development:** The Distance

We would also like to thank the following people for their valuable contribution to writing and developing the material:
Pamela Vittorio (Video Script Writer), Belen Fernandez (App Project Manager), Eleanor Clements (App Content Creator)

We would like to thank all those who have given their kind permission to reproduce material for this book:

**Illustrators:**
Simon Clare; Guillaume Gennet c/o Lemonade; John Goodwin; Sean Longcroft c/o KJA Artists; The Boy Fitzhammond c/o NB Illustration Ltd.

**Photos:**
*J. Escandell.com; J. Jaime; J. Lucas; S. Enríquez;* 123RF; ALAMY/ GerryRousseau, Jim Corwin, Moviestore collection Ltd, Simon Reddy, Stephen French, IanDagnall Computing, Joern Sackermann, dpa picture alliance, Serhii Kucher, ZUMA Press, Inc., All Canada Photos, London Entertainment, Everett Collection Inc, imageBROKER, Pongpun Ampawa, Peter Noyce GBR, Ian Allenden, AF archive, Elizabeth Livermore, Lex Rayton, Ted Foxx, Alvey & Towers Picture Library, Elizabeth Wake, Kristoffer Tripplaar, Lucas Vallecillos, Joe Fairs, Dinodia Photos, Peter D Noyce, Brigette Supernova, Pictorial Press Ltd, Collection Christophel, Jonathan Goldberg, Paul Hastie, Tierfotoagentur, REUTERS, Viktor Fischer, Art of Food, Andrey Armyagov, Alex Ramsay, Blend Images, B Christopher, Judith Collins, David Cabrera Navarro, Roman Tiraspolsky, robertharding, Michael Neelon(misc), Fredrick Kippe, Oleksiy Maksymenko Photography, Patti McConville, D. Callcut, Matthew Taylor, Rafael Angel Irusta Machin, Igor Kovalchuk, Mallorcaimages, Paul Quayle, Jozef Polc, Mick Sinclair, Michael Willis, Hugh Threlfall, ITAR-TASS Photo Agency, Bailey-Cooper Photography, jeremy sutton-hibbert, creativep, James Jeffrey Taylor, Oleksiy Maksymenko, Paul Smith, David Levenson, United Archives GmbH, Justin Kase zsixz, Simon Dack, Jeremy Pembrey, Barry Diomede, Alex Linch, Tomas Abad, Valentin Luggen, Sergey Soldatov, Iakov Filimonov, Anton Gvozdikov, Alex Segre, MBI, Paul Gibson, Stocksolutions, MEDIUM FORMAT COLLECTION/Balan Madhavan, allesalltag, David Robertson, Dmytro Zinkevych, Simon Dack News, Vaidas Bucys; CATERS NEWS AGENCY; FOCOLTONE; GETTY IMAGES SALES SPAIN/bjdlzx, Yuri_Arcurs, Reenya, Nikada, Paul Almasy, Martin Rose,

Maskot, Lars Baron, JamieB, Annie Engel, Fosin2, Darumo, BraunS, artisticco, ajr_images, Bison_, AzmanL, artursfoto, pringletta, Dobino, Berezka_Klo, Indeed, Hero Images, KingWu, Tom Merton, NI QIN, Sam Edwards, Portra, ajaykampani, bgblue, leungchopan, c_kawi, s-c-s, kali9, SensorSpot, LeoPatrizi, Talaj, Pix11, Neyya, Dan Dalton, Chimpinski, DKart, shank_ali, Chris Ryan, londoneye, kickstand, kiankhoon, joto, Fuse, skynesher, asbe, gavran333, Zinkevych, KJA, AFP, ViewStock, John Lund/Sam Diephuis, Hiya Images/Corbis/VCG, Tom Dulat, vm, imaginima, TF-Images, Ben Pipe Photography, Ridofranz, PPcavalry, Edda Dupree / EyeEm, Dave Hogan/MTV 2016, Lightcome, Isovector, VikramRaghuvanshi, FaraFaran, Cimmerian, Bet_Noire, David C Tomlinson, Dave & Les Jacobs, unaemlag, technotr, Zoran Kolundzija, tarras79, stockcam, MacLife Magazine, Jetta Productions, Maya Karkalicheva, DGLimages, innovatedcaptures, FatCamera, Power Sport Images, Jasmina81, Lorraine Boogich, Mirrorpix, Kevin C. Cox - FIFA, Purestock, Caiaimage/Tom Merton, Stockbyte, Jason England / EyeEm, Ted Soqui, scyther5, Steven Swinnen / EyeEm, Weedezign, Westend61, Dave and Les Jacobs/Kolostock, chachamal, Cultura RM Exclusive/Frank and Helena, Echo, imagotres, julief514, karandaev, kpalimski, demaerre, Danny Martindale, Art-Y, omda_info, colematt, clubfoto, Allan Tannenbaum, DNY59, stevecoleimages, David Lees, DonNichols, JB Lacroix, asiseeit, Tuutikka, Tarzhanova, Thinkstock, Vladimir Godnik, Uwe Krejci, Venturelli, VladTeodor, Synergee, NurPhoto, Samuel de Roman, nycshooter, RuslanDashinsky, sorincolac, AndreyPopov, AngiePhotos, MistikaS, JGalione, Choreograph, Fotoplanner, Leah Puttkammer, Hero images, John Keeble, Liam Norris, JANIFEST, LWA/Dann Tardif, Ron Galella, Rose_Carson, IvanMiladinovic, Shana Novak, Simon Sarin, T3 Magazine, Floortje, Hung_Chung_Chih, artlensfoto, domin_domin, Frank van Delft, macrovector, michaeljung, penguenstok, Flashpop, DenisKot, Wavebreakmedia, Creative, Claudiad, Sheikoevgeniya, Philipp Nemenz, Bettmann, Al Freni, EmirMemedovski, wir0man, pshonka, Anthony Harvey, Anadolu Agency, mrak_hr, mixetto, i love images, mbbirdy, kivoart, SnegiriBureau, Rick Friedman, jsnover, iconeer, Monty Rakusen, gilaxia, Maksim Ozerov, gerenme, MStudioImages, MATJAZ SLANIC, andresr, Jupiterimages, Jon Feingersh, adekvat, Jamie Garbutt, Jack Mitchell, Mark Cuthbert, R-O-M-A, Paras Griffin, Peathegee Inc, Radius Images, Gabriel Rossi, FrozenShutter, blueringmedia, davidcreacion, NuStock, justhavealook, reportman1985, zeljkosantrac, Dougal Waters, David Redfern, Askold Romanov, Digital Vision, Krasyuk, Javier Pierini, Marc Romanelli, Neustockimages, Andersen Ross, Alistair Berg, Steven Puetzer, Todor Tsvetkov, Devonyu, franckreporter, Anthony Charles, Danita Delimont, senkoumelnik, ferrantraite, Chesnot, ersinkisacik, bluejayphoto, NicolasMcComber, Photos.com Plus, Robyn Mackenzie, Astarot, Tony Vaccaro, Santiago Felipe, Tristan Fewings, Tetra Images, dogayusufdokdok, nicoletaionescu, praetorianphoto, vgajic, Sofie Delauw, Birgit R / EyeEm, Christopher Polk, PeopleImages, Henn Photography, KavalenkavaVolha, Kittisak_Taramas, tunart, Mike Coppola, Nicolas McComber, Tatjana Kaufmann, LuisPortugal, christopherarndt, Adrian Weinbrecht, Chris Sattlberger, subjug, JuliarStudio, Juice Images, Jrg Mikus / EyeEm, sturti, Roberto Westbrook, Tanya Constantine, Valery Sharifulin, Jason Hawkes, Image Source, IMAGEMORE Co., Ltd., Jacob Wackerhausen, seb_ra, crossroadscreative, m-imagephotography, DEA PICTURE LIBRARY, Hiroyuki Ito, Erik Isakson, EvgeniyaTiplyashina, Hill Street Studios, lushik, Mondadori Portfolio, Andreas Hein / EyeEm, Axelle/ Bauer-Griffin, Emad Aljumah, Deborah Kolb, monkeybusinessimages, Alexandr Sherstobitov, laflor, Michael Ochs Archives, Science Photo Library, BJI / Blue Jean Images, Dan MacMedan, ChrisHepburn, kzenon, Banar Fil Ardhi / EyeEm, PhotoAlto/Sigrid Olsson, Jade Albert Studio, Inc., New York Daily News Archive, Constantinos Kollias / EyeEm, Chris Walter, Photo by Claude-Olivier Marti, Kelly Cheng Travel Photography, Blend Images - Jose Luis Pelaez Inc, shapecharge, Compassionate Eye Foundation/Steven Errico, gbh007; HIGHRES PRESS STOCK/AbleStock. com; I. PREYSLER; ISTOCKPHOTO/ Getty Images Sales Spain, Devasahayam Chandra Dhas, Andreas Herpens, calvindexter, popovaphoto, Phazemedia, denphumi, SolStock, Pali Rao, JoeLena; J. M.ª BARRES; SHUTTERSTOCK/ Glenn Copus/Evening Standard, Olivia Rutherford, MARIUS ALEXANDER, Iakov Filimonov, Sergey Novikov, Blend Images, terekhov igor; Farmer's Daughter; Jono Williams; Andrew Hyde; Aimee Giese; Museum of London; Samsung; SERIDEC PHOTOIMAGENES CD; Telegraph Media Group Limited; ARCHIVO SANTILLANA

**Cover Photo:** GETTY IMAGES SALES SPAIN/mixetto

**We would like to thank the following reviewers for their valuable feedback which has made Personal Best possible. We extend our thanks to the many teachers and students not mentioned here.**
Brad Bawtinheimer, Manuel Hidalgo, Paulo Dantas, Diana Bermúdez, Laura Gutiérrez, Hardy Griffin, Angi Conti, Christopher Morabito, Hande Kokce, Jorge Lobato, Leonardo Mercato, Mercilinda Ortiz, Wendy López

Printed in Brazil by Forma Certa Gráfica Digital

LOTE: 788937